Experiencing the Bible
with Children

Experiencing the Bible with Children

Dorothy Jean FURNISH

ABINGDON PRESS

Nashville

EXPERIENCING THE BIBLE WITH CHILDREN

Furnish, Dorothy Jean, 1921-
    Experiencing the Bible with Children / Dorothy Jean Furnish.
        p.   cm.
    Includes bibliographical references.
    ISBN 0-687-12425-5 (alk. paper)
    1. Bible—Children's use.   I. Title.
BS618.F87   1990
220'.07—dc20   89-49188
                                                            CIP

Scripture quotations unless otherwise noted are from the Revised Standard Version of the Bible, copyright 1946, 1952, 1971, by the Division of Christian Education of the National Council of the Churches of Christ in the USA, and are used by permission.

94 95 96 97 98 99 00 01 02 03 04 — 10 9 8 7 6 5 4

CONTENTS

PREFACE

In the search for ways to help children discover Bible meanings, our starting point is *an understanding of the Bible itself*. Where did the Bible come from? What does it mean to call it the *Word of God*? What does it say? These are some of the questions examined in Section One: The Bible.

In the search for ways to help children discover Bible meanings, we also need *to understand the nature of childhood*. What are children like? What can they understand about religion? Given our understanding of the Bible and the nature of children, how shall the Bible be taught? We begin to deal with these questions in Section Two: The Children.

The goal of Bible study with children is to open the Bible for them in such a way that they are able *to experience the Bible content and discover meaning for their present lives, while keeping open the possibility of future learning and meanings*. Specific ways of doing this are presented in Section Three: The Methods.

This volume is a revision, combination, and condensation of two earlier volumes: *Exploring the Bible with Children* (1975) and *Living the Bible with Children* (1979), both published by Abingdon Press and both now out of print. It is presented in response to needs expressed by directors of Christian education, seminary professors, and denominational and judicatory personnel. The book is also a response to interest shown by church school teachers who have attended workshops led by the author on the theme "Experiencing the Bible with Children."

Acknowledgments are made to former students at Garrett-Evangelical Theological Seminary (Evanston,

Ill.) who contributed to *Living the Bible with Children* and whose work has been revised for inclusion here: Mary Jo Osterman, Carol Johnson Sorenson, and Michael E. Williams. Also acknowledged is permission to reprint a portion of Psalm 14 from *Psalms Anew: In Inclusive Language*, compiled by Nancy Schreck and Maureen Leach (Saint Mary's Press, Winona, Minn., 1986).

D.J.F., 1990

Experiencing the Bible
with Children

SECTION ONE: THE BIBLE

1.
BIBLE BEGINNINGS

The story of how the Bible came to be is much more than a series of dates and descriptions of documents, although these matters are important. Of equal importance is an understanding of the process by which these documents came to be accepted as the Scriptures of the church. This chapter briefly sketches the development of the Bible from the earliest oral traditions to the latest English revisions.

The Oral Tradition

Long before the Bible appeared in written form, many parts of both the Old Testament and the New Testament were passed by word of mouth from village to village and from one generation to the next. Old Testament oral tradition, as it is called, was formed through the repeating of stories or conversations. Some of the stories were about the origins of Israel, the covenant of Israel with God, the Exodus, and the Passover. The liturgical forms of the Old Testament were both part of the oral tradition and carriers of it. Even the laws that came out of the daily life of the community were carried by the oral tradition before they were written into the lawbooks. Before the reign of David, in about the tenth century B.C., there is no evidence of any written documents containing these materials.

Many of the familiar accounts in the New Testament have their origin in an oral tradition also. One of the oldest forms of oral tradition was the *pronouncement story*. When guidance in ethical conduct was needed in the early Christian community, an appropriate personal encounter with Jesus would be recalled and narrated. It would be concluded with a pronouncement to fit the need; for example, "'Render therefore to Caesar the things that are Caesar's, and to God the things that are God's'" (Matthew 22:21).

Another form of the oral tradition was the *miracle story*. When summoning evidence to convince their hearers that Jesus was the Son of God, early Christians would recall stories they had heard of miracles he performed. They would describe the setting and the miraculous act itself. As an ending to the story they would attest to its validity by stating the consequences of the event. For example, the story of the healing of Jairus' daughter concluded with the words, "And immediately the girl got up and walked" (Mark 5:42).

Another of these old forms of the oral tradition was the *sayings of Jesus*. Today we preserve important words with a tape recorder. The followers of Jesus collected his sayings by careful listening and· frequent repetition, preserving them in their memories. One of these collections is known to us as the Sermon on the Mount.

The *parables* of Jesus also illustrate a form of oral tradition. Some scholars say that each parable was intended to call attention to a particular truth; others claim that the real purpose of the parables was to hide a truth until people were ready to understand it. For whatever reason, it is clear that the parable was an appealing form, easily remembered, and often repeated. Even today the parables are favorites among children, who frequently choose them as subject matter for dramatization.

Finally, one of the most familiar forms which the oral tradition took was the *stories about Jesus*, including his birth, temptation, transfiguration, death, and resurrection.

Until about A.D. 50 the oral tradition was the only way in which the life of the early Christian community was preserved. This significant fact means that all the words of Jesus have come to us through an oral tradition. It accounts for the fact that much of the material in the Gospel is in short paragraphs and anecdotes which were easy to remember and repeat. Since our Bible carries accounts of only a small fraction of what must have happened, it indicates that the materials so preserved were seen to be of unusual worth. It suggests that interpretations of events and sayings had taken place even before they were written down. Finally, it demonstrates that the roots of the New Testament are deeply imbedded in the life of the early Christian church.

An understanding of the oral tradition does not allow us to view the Bible as a static document from ancient times. Rather we learn to appreciate the Bible as a dynamic account of living history.

The Written Tradition

Groups that exist long enough to develop self-identity and traditions usually produce historians who in turn produce written records. Somewhere in the line of descendants almost every family has its self-appointed genealogists. Histories are produced by local churches, counties, social groups, and presidents. Preachers gather their sermons into books, and teachers gather their stories into anthologies. It was no different for our Judeo-Christian ancestors. Eventually some of their oral traditions found their way into written form.

Old Testament storytellers began to gather the rich materials which had been told and retold by women at the wells or by men around the campfires. A storyteller from the south of Judah (called "J" by the Old Testament scholars because he calls God "Jehovah" or "Yahweh") wrote his stories approximately 850 B.C.

Nearly one hundred years later another storyteller, this time from the north of Judah, put his stories into writing. (He is called "E" because he refers to God as "Elohim.") These two accounts have been woven together and are found in the Pentateuch, the first five books of the Old Testament. Also to be found there are lawbooks of ancient Israel from the fifth and fourth centuries B.C. known as "D" (Deuteronomic Code) and "P" (Priestly Code). Gradually the rest of the Old Testament was added so that by 200 B.C. all the Old Testament had been written. This was almost seven hundred years after the first known writings. The original language of the Old Testament was Hebrew.

The first written documents of the New Testament are the letters of Paul. Although he must have been familiar with much of the oral tradition, his purpose in writing was not to preserve that tradition. Most of his letters speak directly to the needs of the early Christian churches, especially those in the Gentile world. It is generally agreed that his letter to the Thessalonians is the earliest book in the New Testament, perhaps as early as A.D. 50, and that all of his letters were written before any of the Gospels.

The Gospel of Mark is the earliest written document known to us today which devotes itself to an orderly account of the oral tradition about Jesus. Written by A.D. 65–70, it was followed by Matthew, A.D. 75–85, and Luke, A.D. 85–95. The Gospel of John was written much later, probably between A.D. 100 and 115.

Both the letters of Paul and the Gospels were intended for those who had not personally known Jesus because they lived in a distant place or at a later time. They were written in the language of the marketplace, Koine Greek. By A.D. 150 all the New Testament books were in existence.

Canonization

The Bible was written, piece by piece, over a period of almost twelve hundred years. It is certain there were many other religious writings authored during this same period. How some found their way into the Bible and others did not is explained by the term *canonization*. In *A*

Light to the Nations (p. 29) Norman K. Gottwald defines canonization as "the process by which sacred books are selected, embued with authority, and thus set apart from other religious writings that are either heretical or simply of devotional value." This selection and setting apart of materials of which the Bible is composed occurred in many stages. It was a process that took place both within Judaism (with reference to the portion we know as the Old Testament) and within the Christian church (with reference to both the Old and New Testaments).

In Judaism, the standard for selection of writings to be given the authority of Scripture seems to have been a practical one. A writing was included if it had been found by common agreement to be useful to those seeking to live a righteous life. The final selection of Jewish writings and the official stamp of approval was by a rabbinic assembly in A.D. 90 at Jamnia, a city west of Jerusalem.

The Christian church from the beginning used the Jewish religious writings. Since the church arose before the Jewish canon was closed, all those books circulating in Judaism before the closing of the canon passed into the church. Thus it became necessary for the church to define the Old Testament canon for itself.

The Old Testament scriptures were used more and more by the church, with the conviction that they contained the promise that was fulfilled in Jesus Christ. This was understood as their true meaning and intent. So used and interpreted, their acceptance in the Bible of the church was inevitable.

By A.D. 200 there was general agreement that the Gospels, Acts, and Paul's letters were authoritative writings for the Christian. In his Easter letter of A.D. 367, Athanasius, Bishop of Alexandria, listed for the first time the twenty-seven books now found in the New Testament. Since the end of the fourth century this list has been accepted by most parts of the Christian church. The standards used for selection of New Testament writings are not known specifically, but they seem to have included affirmative answers to these three questions: (1) Was it written by an apostle or someone close to an apostle? (2) Was it used widely by the church in the instruction of converts? (3) Is the authentic tradition presented?

Canonization is the process by which a closed collection of scriptures becomes authorized by the church for use in the churches as the standard for inspiration and teaching.

Translations and Revisions

There are three major incentives for new translations and revisions of the Bible. First is the conviction that all persons should be able to read it in their own language; second is the belief that it is best understood in the contemporary idiom; and third is the never-ending search for increased accuracy in translation. The first two reasons dominated until the nineteenth century. Another surge of interest came with new discoveries of ancient manuscripts and new skill in understanding ancient languages.

Each translation of the Bible and each revision came out of a unique set of circumstances, including technology, politics, doctrinal controversies, and church reform. Translators were exiled, some lost their lives, and others lived out their years in fear because they were responsible for new statements of the Bible text. A sweeping look at the development of the English Bible is presented in "The Making of the English Bible" by Clyde Manschreck in *The Interpreter's One-Volume Commentary on the Bible*.

The journey from oral tradition to the latest edition of the Bible in the English language covers many centuries and depends on countless storytellers, writers, translators, and revisers. In addition to English, the entire Bible has been translated into over 250 different languages and dialects. This continued dedication to a difficult task testifies to the vital place the Bible holds in the history of the world.

2.
A CONFRONTING EVENT

The Bible is central to our understanding of Christianity. The earliest Christians possessed the Old Testament in the form of the Jewish Scriptures. From the very beginning the church knew the valuable oral traditions about the life, death, and resurrection of Jesus. The letters of Paul were read in the churches less than twenty-five years after the death of Jesus. And by A.D. 150 all the writings in the Bible were available.

Throughout all the centuries that followed, people have tried to describe adequately the nature of the Bible, and the resulting interpretations of its meaning have been many. These varied approaches have led to numerous theological positions, hundreds of denominations and sects, a wide range of life-styles, and even bitter conflict between Christians. In spite of all these differences, Christians have given general consent to a description of the Bible, calling it "the Word of God." We recognize that the Bible is uniquely a book about God, but the question remains, in what way is it the Word of God?

This chapter examines six different descriptions of the nature of the Bible. Five are perspectives readily discovered in the course of general Bible study. The sixth is the writer's point of view. In writing about each of the first five approaches there is brief mention of how it influences the way the Bible is taught to children and of its major contributions.

Some Other Perspectives

The Bible as God's Word: Written and Uninterpreted

Some who describe the Bible as the *Word of God* use the term in a literal sense. That is, the Bible contains the actual words of God, faithfully and accurately recorded by the writers. Since God's revelation is through these words, the exact terminology of the biblical text becomes extremely important. Revisions are seen as interpretations and therefore a tampering with the Scriptures. Efforts are not made to understand the text in terms of cultural and historical roots. It is felt that the Word of God can be known through the Bible—and in no other way. Some have a less literal approach but still want to be sure that the Bible as the revelation of God is allowed to speak without interpretation.

When this view of the Bible is held by teachers of children, a certain teaching style emerges. First, the importance of the text itself leads to an emphasis on memorization of Bible verses. These are often chosen for their brevity or ease in memorization. Second, the importance of the text is sometimes taken to mean that all portions of the Bible are equally relevant. It is felt that children can learn a lesson from almost any portion of the Bible. Third, in the use of Bible stories the emphasis is on the details of the story and perhaps its moral application. Fourth, the Bible is sometimes seen as the only text necessary.

A major contribution of those who hold this view is their firm stand that the Bible is unique, that it is the primary source for our understanding of God and as such is essential for Christian faith.

The Bible as an Interpretation of God's Word

The Bible is declared to be God's Word by many who do not hold the view just described. These people acknowledge that *interpretation* of the Bible has occurred since the beginning of the oral tradition. In repeating a story or idea over and over again interpretive words crept in. As persons translated from Hebrew and Greek to Latin and then to several English editions over a period of more than four hundred years, they left in the text traces of their own understanding. By citing Jeremiah 1:1-2, "The Words of Jeremiah . . . to whom the word of the Lord came," one writer suggests that the Bible is a human word which seeks to express God's Word.

Others qualify their concept of the Bible as the Word of God by saying that it is a *record* of God's Word or that it *contains* God's Word. Even though interpretation by storytellers, writers, and translators is conceded, there is still the hope that interpretation may be kept to a minimum. In the effort to recover original texts, the skills of biblical scholarship are employed.

When applied to the teaching of children this view puts emphasis on Bible knowledge, although not necessarily the ability to recall the precise words of the text. Stories and larger segments such as the Ten Commandments, the Sermon on the Mount, and the parables are stressed rather than single verses. To understand the text itself it is thought helpful to have an understanding of the writers, their audience, and the cultural and historical setting in which they lived. Therefore, in addition to the Bible, children use supplementary resources such as maps, concordances, commentaries, and pupils' books containing other background materials.

The major contribution of those who hold this view is the freedom from strict adherence to the text that is possible because of the conviction that Bible writers and translators included some of their own understanding.

The Bible as a Sourcebook

Some who refer to the Bible as a *sourcebook* see it as a book about human beings rather than a book about God. To call it the Word of God is to set it apart from other books. Its uniqueness lies in the particular set of events it describes, not in the special quality of the events.

As a sourcebook the Bible has religious and nonreligious value. To the extent that its events and dates can be scientifically verified, the Bible is of interest to historians and political scientists. Sociologists and anthropologists study its tribal organization, religious rites, descriptions of villages and cities, and customs and mores of its people. Students of literature and language development appreciate it as an important resource. According to one Bible scholar, those who use the Bible in these ways see it as a "literary artifact to unlock the mystery of the times."

Others see the Bible as a unique sourcebook for Christians. It not only contains information about the past, but also provides answers to the problems of living in today's world. Although some would say that answers to all questions can be found in the Bible and that no other source is necessary, most would agree that the Bible is only one of many sources to which persons may go to find solutions for problems. In either case, the Bible is read as some would read an encyclopedia rather than as one would read a story.

There are two ways church school teachers use the Bible as a sourcebook. Those who see it as a source for rules of conduct and answers to life's problems make frequent reference to the Ten Commandments, the Golden Rule, the Sermon on the Mount, and selections from the letters of Paul. Sometimes a Bible reference will open up discussion of a child's question or problem. More often the immediate need is discussed first, and then a commonsense solution is found and validated by reference to the Bible. Teachers who see the Bible as only one resource book among many use it to stimulate thinking, give information, and provide one perspective which can then be compared with others. In this case many other reference books are made available to be used in the same way. Since it is a sourcebook, children are taught how to find portions of the Bible they wish to use.

A major contribution of the sourcebook view is the conviction that Bible study simply for its own sake is not enough. For the Bible to have any meaning for the reader it must speak to a need for information or deal with some of life's persistent concerns.

The Bible as a History of God's People

The ordinary people of Israel became extraordinary as they came to see themselves as God's people. The Bible is sometimes described as a *history* of God's people. It is seen as an account of important people and events, often replete with specific dates and places. Unlike the sourcebook view, however, this history is unique because through it God has chosen to be known.

The history of the Judeo-Christian tradition is of special interest to Christians, perhaps in the same way that study of American history is of interest to Americans. To maintain our identity as a nation, it is important that we be reminded from time to time of our historical origins. References might be made to the American Revolution, the Constitution, and the words of Washington and Jefferson. Similarly, Christianity is better understood when people are reminded of the Creation; the Exodus; the words of the Prophets; the birth, death, and resurrection of Jesus; and the beginnings of the Christian church.

The Bible is seen as unique history, however, because through this history God is revealed. God's Word was spoken to a particular group of people, at a particular time, and within a particular cultural setting. God's Word is the same now as it was then. Therefore, through the understanding and interpretation of this history, God's Word is known to us today.

Those who teach from this view have a special interest in Bible customs, geography, and the sequence of events. Anxious that children know Bible customs, teachers display Bible pictures that have been painted only after careful research or they help children make Palestinian villages. If drama is used, care is taken to make costumes, scenic background, and props as authentic as possible. Because a knowledge of the geography is necessary, map study is carried out using wall charts, atlases, globes, or detailed relief maps made by the children. Since the sequence of historical events is important, children learn dates, places, and names by memorization or by the creation of time lines.

One major contribution of this approach is the conviction that to understand the Bible it is necessary to have an understanding of the cultural and historical setting in which it was written.

The Bible as a Witness to Divine-Human Encounter

Three of the four concepts of the Bible which have been presented so far describe God as the most active participant in the Divine-human relationship. In these views God spoke to the people of Israel through the events of their history, and God speaks to us today through the written record of these events in the Bible. The expectation of response on the part of God's listeners has not been obvious, although it may have been implied.

When viewing the Bible as a *witness to Divine-human encounter*, we observe three new elements:

First, this approach introduces the human being as an active participant in God's history. The concern is not only with the Word but with human response to that Word. The Bible is not only a book about God; it is a book about the way people have responded to God.

Second, this approach to the Bible introduces the dimension of encounter. An encounter between two persons is not usually a casual meeting, although the dictionary gives that as one meaning of the word. It is more often an intense relationship which is not quickly forgotten. It is a give-and-take in which each makes demands on the other with such insistence that they cannot be ignored. The Bible tells of this kind of interaction and struggle between God and persons. It is more than a history of events. And it is more than God speaking and people responding. The Bible is a witness to Divine-human encounter.

The third new element in this approach is indicated by the word *witness*. The Bible was written by witnesses to this history of encounter between God and people. Because the witnesses were participants in the encounter, it cannot be an objective history. They interpreted God's Word in the light of their own response to that Word.

An understanding of the Bible as a witness to Divine-human encounter adds new possibilities for the teacher of children. Since the people of the Bible themselves take on added significance, the teacher plans activities that will make these people come alive. Many of the activities used by those who view the Bible as a "history of God's people" are just as appropriate here. But time lines, pictures, maps, and Palestinian villages cannot adequately describe what it is like to have an encounter with God! The teacher is interested in helping children understand the feelings of Bible persons. For example, the parable of the prodigal son might be acted out with an emphasis on the emotional responses of the characters. Or children might make puppets and use them to portray the feelings of the wise men and the shepherds.

The first purpose of all these activities is to help children know how it felt to be the human side of the Divine-human encounter. The second purpose is to help children discover what the people of the Bible learned about God. This is seen by some to be the most important result of the teaching because it is through the experiences of Bible persons that we know what God is like.

The major contribution of this approach is the conviction that the Bible is not a book just about God but that it is a book about the encounter between God and persons, written by witnesses who were also participants.

The Bible: A Confronting Event

The concept of the Bible as a *confronting event* does not stand in total opposition to the five views just presented, but it builds on the major contributions of each. While leaning most heavily on the understanding of the Bible as a witness to Divine-human encounter, this concept adds elements of its own.

The Bible Is an Event

There is a difference between talking about the "events" recorded in the Bible and describing the Bible as an "Event." The events in the Bible are sometimes observable bits of history such as battles, births, deaths, shipwrecks, political intrigues, famines, floods, or baptisms. Sometimes these events are persons: Abraham, Sarah, Isaac, Rebekah, Jacob, Moses, the prophets, the disciples, Jesus, Mary, or Paul. Sometimes events are interpreted in such a meaningful way that the interpretations themselves become events—for example, the stories of Creation, the messages of the prophets, the pronouncements of the Gospel writers, or the theology of Paul. Sometimes events are experiences or happenings such as the conversion of Paul or the song of Miriam. It is through these events and others like them that God has been made known.

In the same way that a letter from Paul was an event in the lives of the early Christians who heard it read in the churches, the Bible can be an event in the lives of Christians today. Although it is sixty-six distinct books and therefore might properly be referred to as sixty-six events, the church has selected them as uniquely valuable for Christians. These books, together known to us as the Bible, have become one book with its own identity and its own life. This book gathers all the events recorded in each of the books, and, as a collection of history, interpretations, persons, and experience, it becomes itself another event to be understood, another event through which persons can discover God. And because it is synonymous with the Bible, we spell this event with a capital *E* and call the Bible an Event.

The Bible Is a "Now" Event

The first five perspectives described the Bible largely in the past tense. The Bible contains words written long ago; it tells of events that occurred in another age; it is a sourcebook which contains a history of an ancient people; it witnesses to Divine-human encounters that took place in the past.

We limit the Bible if we see it only as a record of something that happened long ago. As an Event it has within itself the power to bring the past into the present in such a spectacular way that the Bible becomes a "now" Event in the lives of persons today. It is an event through which God seeks to be known to us just as he became known through the events of the past to which it witnesses.

The Bible Brings About Encounter

It is the testimony of Christians through the ages that the Bible is not something that can be taken or left alone. Just as the events recorded in the Bible confronted the people who participated in them, so the Bible as an Event confronts us here and now. The Bible is not only a record of Divine-human encounters in the past, but by its very nature it has the power to bring God and persons together in encounters today. When we willingly open ourselves to it, we risk opening to ourselves, to one another, and to God in such a way that we cannot escape a Divine-human encounter. Because the Bible brings about Divine-human encounter, it can be called a "confronting" Event.

The Bible: A Channel for God's Word

The idea of the Bible as the Word of God is so much a part of the history of the Christian church that it must be dealt with in some way by everyone who attempts to describe its nature. Some people see the Bible text itself as the Word of God; others find God's Word in an interpretation of the events of history; still others discover it in the midst of the Divine-human encounters written about in the Bible.

If the Bible is best described as a confronting Event, how is this Event to be understood as the Word of God? Many have struggled with the question, Does a tree falling in a forest make any sound if no one is there to hear it fall? We know that falling trees make a noise because we have the word of those who have been there. To wonder about the presence of sound in the absence of hearers is an intriguing question, but for most of us the answer leads to no important consequence. The crucial observation to make about falling trees is the fact that if we are in the forest when one falls, we jump! And as we jump we say, "What a noise that makes!" Our experience in the forest will make it very difficult for us to ever imagine a tree falling in utter silence.

Is the Bible the Word of God if no one reads it or if it is read as only history or a sourcebook? It is the testimony of the Christian church that in some way it can be understood to be God's Word. To debate what it means to call it the Word of God is for most of us an empty exercise. The crucial observation about the Bible lies in the fact that if we approach it in such a way that we allow it to confront us, we must respond. And one way we respond is to say, "Surely the Bible must be the Word of God!" Our experience with the Bible will make it very difficult for us to ever think about it without in some way describing it as God's Word.

God and persons have been engaged in confrontation and response since the beginning of the human race. Some of the witnesses to these events have written their observations and interpretations. These reflections, along with other writings, were selected by the church to become its authorized Scriptures. The Bible not only describes events of Divine-human encounter in the past, but is itself a confronting Event which can enable persons today to enter into meaningful relationships with God. And those who respond when confronted experience it to be for them the Word of God.

More difficult than describing the nature of the Bible is the task of answering the question: Can the Bible be for children a confronting Event? And if so, how?

3.
OPEN TO NEW MEANINGS

The search for an adequate statement of the Bible message is a constant one. To say that the Bible is a confronting Event describes its nature, but it says nothing about the message one can expect to receive because of the confrontation that has taken place. The question crying to be answered is, What does the Bible say? In an effort to voice their understanding of the Bible, some persons have tried to discover a central theme that runs throughout the entire book. There is no unanimous agreement, however, about such a theme because persons bring to their study of the Bible their own past experiences, their own needs, and their own religious beliefs. Those readers who do agree on a central theme often have widely varying interpretations of its meaning. This diversity is no cause for surprise or anxiety. The Bible writers themselves understood and interpreted the events of their times in different ways. The unity of the Bible is to be found in its witness that Divine-human encounter is possible, not in a single explanation of what this encounter means.

In the section that follows, three biblical themes are presented, along with a few of the ways each has been interpreted and some of the ways each might affect the method by which children are taught the Bible. In the concluding section of this chapter the writer shares her own approach to the question, What does the Bible say?

All four statements stand within the Christian tradition. No one of them should be seen as right or wrong, but together they give additional evidence that the Bible holds meaning for those who allow themselves to be confronted by it.

Some Bible Themes

People Are in Trouble

This people-are-in-trouble theme is found in both the Bible and the modern world. The psalmist commented:

> Yahweh looks down from heaven
> to see if there are any who are wise,
> any who worship God.
> But they have all gone astray;
> they are all equally bad.
> Not one of them does what is right,
> not a single one. (Psalm 14:2, 3)[1]

In the midst of World War II, Elton Trueblood wrote, "Something has gone wrong with our civilization." He called the problem and his book *The Predicament of Modern Man*. Although many see this same predicament as a central theme of the Bible, they often describe it in different ways.

Some say that people are in trouble because they are sinners in need of salvation. This is a theological way of talking about the predicament. One view is that people are born good, but that by their actions or the influence of a corrupt society they fall away and become sinners. Another view is that all people are born sinners and can be nothing else. In either case, the way out of the dilemma is only through God's salvation.

Others say people are in trouble because of alienation. We are alienated from one another through personal misunderstandings. Pollution, space travel, energy crises, crime, and nuclear wars have made us feel like aliens in our world. Perhaps more seriously, we are even alienated

[1]Reprinted from *Psalms Anew: In Inclusive Language*, compiled by Nancy Schreck and Maureen Leach (Winona, Minn.: Saint Mary's Press, 1986). Used by permission of the publisher. All rights reserved.

from ourselves. These are psychological explanations of our predicament. We are in need of reconciliation, wholeness, and mental health; one writer calls this need "wholth."

Still others would remind us that being in trouble is the story of our collective lives. In his play *The Skin of Our Teeth*, Thornton Wilder portrays with humor the struggle for survival that has gone on ever since the creation of the world. Whenever the human race has just about extricated itself from the ashes of a great calamity, a new catastrophe befalls it! So we have gone from famine to flood to plague to war to who knows what will happen next? This is a historical explanation of our predicament. Somehow we need to find a way to break out of this pattern.

Our understanding of the theme of predicament, both its importance and its meaning, will influence the goals and teaching methods used in the Christian education of children. If sinfulness is stressed, the Bible may be used as a doorway to conversion or as a set of "Thou shalt nots." If alienation is the interpretation chosen, there may be more importance placed on the quality of the interpersonal relationships between teachers and children than on the quantity of Bible material. If our predicament is seen largely as a struggle for survival, there will in all likelihood be an emphasis on community, national, and worldwide concerns.

Although interpretations of its meaning vary, the people-are-in-trouble theme is widely held as central to the biblical message.

God Acts in History

The people-are-in-trouble theme focuses its attention on the plight and activity of persons. In contrast, God is the central figure for those who say the Bible can be understood best if we see it as a testimony that God has acted throughout our history. To say this is to dispute some other popular notions about God. For instance, emphasis on the activity of God in history is a denial of the idea that at the time of creation God wound up the world and then turned it loose to run on its own. Nor is it possible to see God as a judge who sits apart watching the activities of people, immobile until appealed to for help. Rather, the Bible is a record of God's ongoing creative activity in the world. The fact that God has acted in history is important because we can assume that God is active in our history too.

Those who contend that God's action in history is the central theme of the Bible characterize this action through a variety of descriptive terms. Only two will be mentioned.

First, there are those who see God as active in the "saving events" of our Judeo-Christian tradition. This obviously builds on the people-are-in-trouble theme since people need to be rescued from personal or cosmic disaster. These saving events include, among others, God's call and God's promises to Abraham; God's deliverance of Israel from slavery; and the life, death, and resurrection of Jesus Christ. The emphasis here is on particular events in which we see God's saving activity.

Second, there are those who stress not only the events themselves but the relationship between these events— the dependency they have on one another. Bernhard Anderson, in his book *The Unfolding Drama of the Bible,* has given us the imagery of God's action in history as a historical drama with three acts. The use of drama ties the events together with a beginning and an ending. God is the central figure in the play, the Director, the Prompter in the wings, and the Chief Actor on the stage. The "program" looks like this:

> Prologue: Creation
> Act I: Scene 1—Encounter with God
> Scene 2—Discipline and Disaster

Act II: Scene 1—The Second Exodus
          Scene 2—People of the Law

Act III: Scene 1—Victory Through Defeat
          Scene 2—Church and World

Epilogue: History's Finale

The drama of the Bible begins with Creation and rapidly unfolds as other events follow. In act I, scene 1, the encounter of God with humanity takes place in the events of the Exodus, in the call to Moses, in the covenant promise, and in the designation of the Jews as a chosen people. Scene 2 describes the rise and fall of Israel and God's judgment. Act II, scene 1 tells the story of the Babylonian exile and the deliverance from it by God's action. The response in terms of becoming the "people of the Law" is shown in scene 2. The climax of the drama is in act III, scene 1. Here the Christ event is depicted as victory through defeat. The results of this victory appear in scene 2. They are Pentecost, God's new creation—the church—and the beginnings of the gospel spread into all the world. The epilogue is the affirmation that the biblical drama has been moving toward a goal and that the goal is the working out of God's purpose in the world. It is in the epilogue that we catch a vision of the coming kingdom of God, a time when persons are restored to the "peace, unity, and blessedness" which God intends for them.

Variations of this theme are possible by choosing one of the events as a theme within a theme. For example, another way of speaking of God's action in history is to refer specifically to the covenant relationship written about in Exodus 24:7-8 and then to interpret the entire Bible as the working out of this covenant.

If the Bible is primarily a guide to understanding that God works in history, teachers will not teach the Bible as isolated bits of fact. Rather, they will help children grasp the broad outline of Bible history, stressing at each point God's activity. In addition they will interpret the Bible as evidence that God continues to be active in the affairs of the world today.

Whether understood as saving events, an unfolding drama, or the story of a promise, the common theme is that God has been and continues to be active in all of history.

God Acts Uniquely Through Jesus Christ

The message of the Bible is understood in yet another way. The Bible is not merely evidence that God acts in history, but it is first and foremost a declaration that in the historic events surrounding the person of Jesus, God acted in a unique way. Some people refer to this cluster of events as the "Christ event." So important is this Christ event that the Bible cannot be understood apart from it. The Old Testament is building toward it and must be interpreted in its light. The New Testament owes its existence to it.

The centrality of Jesus Christ to the New Testament and to the Christian faith is unquestioned. How he is the central theme of the Old Testament is less obvious, but can be understood best if the drama imagery is used again. In this case, Jesus Christ is the main character. To leave the theater at the end of act I would be to hear God's promise but miss the most amazing way in which the promise was fulfilled—in the person of Jesus. To leave the theater at the end of act II would be to witness the deliverance of the Jews from slavery in Babylon, only to see them become slaves of their own preoccupation with the law. It is only in act III that their ultimate source of freedom is revealed. Through acts I and II (the Old Testament), players and audience alike know the script. They have seen the "cast of characters in the order of their appearance" and know that the eventual coming of a Messiah or "savior" is in act III. It is this faith with which the actors in the first two acts live and interpret the events of their history.

This theme offers a wealth of biblical materials for use in teaching children. There are stories told by Jesus, especially the parables, and there are the collections of his sayings. There are the stories told about Jesus—stories of his birth, his family, his work, his travels, his friends, his relationship to the religious leaders of his time, and his death and resurrection. Some teachers combine this theme with the people-are-in-trouble theme and stress the saving nature of Christ through whom God is acting now. Here the Bible may be used to impress upon children the urgency of commitment. Others combine this with the God-acts-in-history theme and underscore the fact that God acted by creating Jesus, a real person, who lived at a particular time and did and taught certain specific things. These teachers may use the Bible to show that we can learn how to live as Christians by observing how he lived and learning from what he taught.

If people are in trouble, and if God acts through history, then God acting through Jesus Christ to save the people is a summary of the Bible message, and Jesus Christ is the embodiment of that message.

The Bible: Meanings to Discover

When the question is asked, "What does the Bible say?" it is usually assumed that the answer will be given as if the question had been, "What does the Bible say to everyone in every age?" Or perhaps a note of "ought-ness" creeps in when the answer is given as if the original question had been, "What should everyone hear the Bible say?" A better approach might be to divide the question into two parts: First, "What does the Bible say to everyone?" and second, "What does the Bible say to me?" The rest of this chapter addresses itself to these two questions.

What the Bible Says to Everyone

There are some who seek to answer the question in terms of a single, definitive theme. These attempts can be helpful as contributions to our thinking, although universal acceptance of any one of them is unlikely. Even if such agreement were possible, there are good reasons why it should not be our goal. In the first place, the writers of the Bible ought to be allowed to speak for themselves. To interpret their words under the umbrella of some overarching theme may be to impose upon them a point of view with which they would not agree. Rather than limiting their witness in this way, we should rejoice in the richness of their diverse testimony which, taken as a whole, becomes an Event with power to engage us in an encounter with God.

In the second place, times change. Although the Bible is a timeless document, it is understood differently at different times. In the early part of this century the possibility of a people-are-in-trouble theme was quite remote. It did not become popular until the sobering experiences of the Great Depression followed almost immediately by World War II. We have not been bound by past interpretations of the Bible message; similarly, future generations will not allow us to limit their understanding by insistence on one particular theme.

All this is not to say that the Bible does not "speak." It is only to say that its message is in the form of an invitation rather than a final statement. The Bible says to everyone, "Here I am. In me there is possibility of meaning for you. Discover it!" An affirmative answer to this invitation indicates our willingness to be confronted by the Bible. As we respond to that confrontation the meanings we each discover belong to us in a special way. They need not, and probably will not, be expressed in the same way as meanings discovered by others. But it is the personal ownership of the meaning that gives it enough vitality so that it can make a difference in our lives.

There is a danger that this kind of approach to the discovery of Bible meanings will become too individualistic. It is necessary that we avoid falling into the trap of saying, "It doesn't matter what you believe, just so you believe something." This is less likely to happen if emerging understandings are explored and tested in the company of others who have embarked on the same search. It is appropriate, therefore, that the Christian community be the place where we hear and respond to the invitation to discover biblical meanings. The Bible grew out of the witness of the early Christian community; the writings preserved in our Bible were selected by this community; the Christian community, therefore, can serve as a corrective to personal interpretations.

Another Bible Meaning: The "For Us-ness" of God

If the answer to the first question ("What does the Bible say to everyone?") is "Here I am—discover my meaning," how shall we answer the second question, "What does the Bible say to me?" Simply to restate the conviction that each person must discover the meaning for himself/herself and thus bypass the question altogether would be a cop-out. Therefore, in addition to the three themes previously described, the writer offers a fourth theme. Whatever statement the reader makes in response to the question will become a possible fifth theme.

The Bible clearly affirms that God is *for* us. Throughout the succession of events recorded in the Bible, active concern for all persons is made plain. It takes many forms but shows itself primarily in the ways God acts. God gives, withholds, takes away; God threatens, pleads, punishes, approves, shows mercy, loves. God has high hopes for us and confidence in us. God is for us and against anything that diminishes us. Even when we really foul things up the reality of God's "for us-ness" holds out to us the possibility of new life.

Jesus Christ is the most dramatic evidence of God's

"for us-ness." He is both the messenger and the message. It is as if God has pulled out all the stops at once in an effort to convince us of our own worthiness.

Admittedly this is an optimistic point of view, but the Bible is an optimistic book. It witnesses to the fact that God is devoted to developing the potential of all humanity.

God's past actions have been witnessed to by the Bible writers. But God still acts among us. We, too, are witnesses to this activity in the world. There are meanings still to be discovered. It is valid to look at both our history and our present in the search for these meanings. It is important to open the Bible to children in such a way that the past holds out meanings for the present and possibilities of new meanings in the future.

SECTION TWO: THE CHILDREN

4.
UNDERSTANDING TODAY'S CHILDREN

Two major factors affect the development of every child. First is the being itself that is born into the world. It comes with some physical characteristics already determined by the genes inherited from its parents. It arrives equipped with a sexual identity and a racial identity. But, second, at the moment of birth, it encounters the world and the expectations with which it must learn to cope.

While in broad terms it is the same world for all children, in reality each child is born into a particular world, different from that belonging to anyone else. A first child lives in a very different family, for instance, from the brother or sister born several years later. The interplay between this unique being and his or her unique world makes it inevitable that each child will develop in his or her own unique way.

Today's children are not only unique as individuals in relation to one another, but as a generation they are unique from every other generation of children that has ever lived, because the world into which they were born is so strikingly different from the world of any other generation.

Some readers will protest that the world is always in the process of transition, and in this respect today's children are no different from the young of any other era. Yet almost every bone of society's body aches as it never has before from the pressure of rapid change. We may be too close to these changes and too personally involved to understand fully either the causes or the results. A descriptive and comparative word picture of how it seems may be the best we can do.

An Unknown Future

The unpredictability of the future may be one of the most significant ways in which our world differs from other times. Margaret Mead points out that a few generations ago children could visualize their future adulthood by watching their grandparents. Now parents and grandparents find their own life-styles influenced by the life-styles of the young. The continuity between past and future seems to be broken, resulting in an uncertain present and an unpredictable future.

Society's Institutions Are Questioned

It has been customary for sociologists to cite three primary institutions of society: the family, the church, and the school. The structures and values of these institutions provided the stability which made orderly change possible. Although each of them has undergone radical reconstruction from time to time, it is difficult to recall another period when all three have been called into question simultaneously.

The Family: For many children the unity of extended or nuclear families has been replaced by divided families or single-parent homes. For some young adults the concept of legal marriage itself is being questioned. Others have discovered in communal living a new kind of extended family. When talking about family today, no particular organization of persons can be assumed.

The Church: The church, too, is feeling the pressure of change. A church building may stand at the center of some towns and villages, but rarely is it still the center around which the entire community life is organized. Although there have always been critics outside the church, more and more they seem to be within the institution itself.

The Public School: The institution of the public school

is being challenged by both professional educators and local citizens. Criticism with a view to improving the schools is not new. What is new is the serious suggestion that the whole concept of schooling as we know it, from grade school to college, may be ineffective in today's world and therefore obsolete.

Violence: A Way of Life

Until recent years, violence was something that happened someplace else to someone else. Wars were fought abroad. Now, through the miracle of television, they are fought nightly in the living rooms and dining rooms of our country. The same newscasts bring vivid word and picture descriptions of violence close at hand. Gangs are at work in our communities and profiting from the drug business. While violence is viewed by some children on television only, other children are experiencing it firsthand. Guns are purchased by children, and murders committed by fourteen-year-olds or pre-adolescents are becoming more frequent. Children and adults alike seem to have become immune to the horrors of violence.

People Come in Many Colors

Only a few short years ago all North American children lived in a white world, acknowledged to be so by those of all races. Today children live in a multicolored world. Through the efforts of the African American community, black children learn to say and feel the words, "Black is beautiful!" Children in Mexican, Puerto Rican, Native American, and other communities gain new respect for their history and origins, and white children are learning this, too. White is no longer considered best, nor is it a mark of Christian virtue to say, "I never notice a person's color; I see only the person." In today's world, to see persons is to see their color. Many parents and teachers have little personal experience with which to help children cope with the demands that these changes bring.

Changing Sex Roles

"Little boys grow up to be fathers who leave home every morning and go to work. Little girls grow up to be mothers who stay home, take care of the house and the children, and wait for father to come home to dinner." Not too many years ago this statement would have gone unchallenged as an idea, if not a reality. But there is a new wind blowing today, and in some places that wind has reached gale proportions. Where wives engage in work outside the home, more and more husbands are accepting a share of the child-care and household responsibilities. Many women are no longer satisfied with the secretarial, teacher, or nurse image of the employed woman, but aspire to positions of management or acceptance in traditionally male vocations such as truck drivers, police officers, or ordained ministers. In turn, men are more free to become nurses, kindergarten teachers, or secretaries. Although the effects of this trend cannot be fully predicted, there is no doubt that it will have a profound influence on children growing up today.

Life-Work Concept Obsolete

"What are you going to be when you grow up?" is no longer an appropriate way to begin a conversation with a child. With changing technology and social structures, children cannot know the variety of occupations that will be available to them when they are ready to join the work force. Furthermore, if the question is posed at all, it would be more accurate to ask, "What are you going to be *first* when you grow up? And then what? And then what?" The same forces in society which create new occupations can now make current occupations obsolete within the lifetime of an individual. Some who began their careers as test pilots learned new skills so that they could meet the challenges of space as astronauts. Now some of these persons, because of budget cutbacks by the federal government, are finding the third career of their lifetime in the private sector. The child of today who says "I'm going to be a librarian and an engineer and a computer programmer" may not be indecisive—just realistic.

The World Is Getting Bigger

Through modern transportation and communication techniques, the time it takes to reach the other side of the globe, or to convey a message across thousands of miles, has been shortened. Rather than having a small part of the world with which to deal, children must now come to terms in some way with the entire world, including both the earth and all it contains and the space in which it rides. It is no longer possible to withhold information from a child for presentation at some later, more appropriate time.

The Knowledge Explosion

If the right questions were chosen for a test in any subject, the most learned scholar in the field would make a poor showing. Information in every area is being amassed at such a rapid rate it is impossible for one person to know everything about anything, let alone know a great deal about everything. In spite of this, most educational systems are still built on the premise that the retention of information is the primary goal. For children experiencing the knowledge explosion, this is a goal that can lead only to frustration. Although information will always be valuable, and some absolutely necessary, the ability to retrieve information from libraries and computers will be even more important. Persons in this new world can no longer be expected to be storehouses of all knowledge. They must learn how to use other storehouses.

Church school teachers of children are often asked to get down on their knees in order to see a classroom from the eye level of a child. If we cannot grow up in the children's world, the least we can do is try to understand the world in which they are growing up.

5.
THE DEVELOPMENT OF THE CHILD

If we take the fact of a changing world seriously, we are faced with a dilemma, because many of the theories that describe what children are like were developed in a pre-Space Age, pre-Electronic Age, and pre-Atomic Age.

Furthermore, most of these theories were based on studies of a male population with unresearched assumptions that the findings were true for both men and women. Can we be sure that these theories describe the children of today's world? The need is for new theories to be developed on the basis of research done in a new world.

In the meantime there is much we can learn from the research of the twentieth century and from our own careful observations of the children we know. The rest of this chapter reviews some of the things we know about children in general, although they may not be precisely true for any child in particular.

Physical, Social, and Emotional Development

Some of the physical, social, and emotional aspects of a child's development are especially relevant for those who work with children. (Age-group terminology is used in this way: preschool, ages 2-5; early elementary, grades 1-3; and late elementary, grades 4-6.)

Energy Level

It takes a great deal of energy to grow from infancy to adolescence and then to adulthood. Since growth takes place in spurts, the energy level is uneven, too. By the time children reach the preschool years the rapid growth of their earliest years has slowed enough that their energy level is high. They expend this energy in large muscle activities—running, jumping, kicking, throwing—all accompanied by noisemaking. Their attention span, if they are really involved, may be only five to fifteen minutes in length. Often it is much shorter. Their exhaustion is finally evidenced by irritability and restlessness, sometimes even as they persist in the activity. This high level of energy continues into the elementary years. It shows itself not only in physical activity, but in the capacity for great enthusiasm about a project of special interest, or in the ability of late elementary children to argue endlessly!

As the later elementary years arrive, those who are approaching puberty will begin to tire more easily. This is especially noticeable in girls since they mature earlier than boys. It means a great variation in the energy levels between children in any group, and in most cases a variation in energy level for a given child from one day to the next.

But what if you have asthma or are hooked on drugs or are always tired because your folks yell at each other all night and you can't sleep or because no one is home to get your supper, so you eat French fries at the drive-in most of the time?

Interaction with Significant Persons

Children become persons as they relate to other persons whom they consider to be important. The most significant person in the infant's life is the one who has primary responsibility for its care. Usually this is the mother or father, although it may be an older child in the family, a grandparent, or an employed caretaker. Soon other members of the family become significant persons, until by the late preschool years neighborhood friends have assumed an important place in the life of the child. When children enter school the range of important persons quickly enlarges, so that approval is sought not only from adults in the family and neighborhood but from children their own age as well. This peer approval becomes more and more crucial as they grow older, until by the end of childhood, adult approval, although still needed, is not as sought after as acceptance by one's own peers.

Interaction with other children begins with play. It is through play that children test their skills and their ability to relate to other human beings. At first the play is not *with*, but *in the presence of,* other children, described therefore as *parallel play.* Playing together cannot occur until children are ready to interact with one another on an equal basis, in contrast to the adult-child kind of interaction they have known before. Learning to play cooperatively is one of the tasks of the later preschool years.

Boys and girls play together in the early elementary years. Late elementary boys begin to form gangs, and girls of the same age tend to break into groups of two or three special friends. Although the friendships are off and on, there is a great loyalty to one another when they are on. Sexual interest today seems to appear earlier than formerly, although it is difficult to know how much of this is the influence of our culture and how much of it is actual biological change.

Children move from saying "I am you" (identity with the dominant parent figure), to "I am me" (beginning of self-identity), to "I want to know you" (beginning of the socialization process), to "I like you" or "I don't like you" (development of discrimination and values). Meaningful relationships with the significant persons at each age are essential.

But what if your parents are divorced and each has remarried, you have brothers and sisters you haven't seen, your grandparents live a thousand miles away, your mother doesn't let you play with the kids on your block because they aren't the "right kind," you are bused to a school three miles in one direction, you go to a church three miles in the opposite direction?

Dependence and Independence

One of the most important tasks of childhood is the move from total dependence on parents toward the ability to care for and make decisions for oneself. It is only when children achieve some degree of autonomy that they are able to assume responsibility for their actions.

Older preschool children have achieved a degree of independence as far as caring for their physical needs is concerned. Toilet and eating habits are generally under control by the time they enter public school kindergarten. Buttons, zippers, shoe laces, bows, and overshoes are in the process of being conquered. This ability makes it possible for children to be more mobile. They can visit friends overnight, attend school, and generally experiment with longer and longer separation from parents.

As children progress through the elementary years they grow increasingly independent in both action and thought, but not without effort and risk. At times it is parents and teachers who hold children back or push them too quickly. At times it is children who are afraid to break away or want to break away all at once. Adults must often seem inconsistent to children at one moment saying, "You'll have to learn to do it yourself, I'm busy!" and at the next moment. "Don't try to do that yourself! You're too little!" This pulling and tugging results in rapid strides toward independence as well as times of slipping back temporarily to the dependence of an earlier age. Both responses are normal and should be expected.

This sense of independence grows throughout the elementary years so that a child moves from pleading, "I can't do it!" to "Please, Mother, I'll do it myself!" and sometimes on to, "Here, I'll do it for you!"

But what if you are in a wheelchair or are blind or your parents are afraid to let you try new things or you are the baby in the family and no one ever lets you do anything for yourself?

Sense of Right and Wrong

The moral judgment of children is related to their sense of independence, their development as responsible persons, and their desire for approval from the significant persons in their lives. It is these persons who provide them with a large part of their value systems. Children learn that some behavior wins approval and some does not. In their circle of important persons, some attitudes are acceptable and some are not. Older preschool children can tell the difference between the acceptable and the unacceptable, especially when it is reinforced by adult approval or disapproval, although they do not always act accordingly.

In the early elementary years children are especially concerned about the question of right and wrong. Fairness emerges as a criterion for judging behavior. Is the punishment fair? Are their friends fair when they play together? Does everyone get an equal share when the snacks are divided? In order to assure that fairness will reign, children of this age become ardent rule-makers. This is a behavior that does not seem to be learned from adults, but is common to children everywhere apparently as a result of solidarity among the children themselves. On occasion the rule-making itself becomes the game and occupies more time than the game for which the rules must be made. Often children will change the rules to suit their own personal advantage, but they do not abandon the concept of rules.

For children in the later elementary years the question of moral judgment begins to shift from What is fair, especially in the behavior of others? to What is right for me to do? It may not always be articulated, and actions may seem to belie the assertion, but in their inner selves children are their own worst critics. When they do not measure up to their own expectations they easily become discouraged.

But what if you always seem to lose when you play by the rules or your friend's mother lets her do things you aren't allowed to do or your father tells you to help him watch for police cars when you are out for a drive or you get scolded when you do something wrong, but no one ever notices when you do something right?

Feelings and Their Expression

Children use their feelings as orchestra members use their instruments, playing them in different ways on different occasions. This makes a live symphony concert more exciting than a recording, and live children more intriguing (and usually more exasperating!) than a book about them.

Emotions are often private, usually elusive, and always changing, so that this aspect of childhood is one of the most difficult to define. Because of the difference in rate of growth and the influence of each child's particular social, mental, and physical growth pattern, there is probably less uniformity in this area than in any of the others. Furthermore, most studies of emotions have dealt with strong motivating emotions such as rage and fear, but not with the more positive affection and joy.

Infant emotions are in response to external factors. Experimentation has shown that by the time children are two years old they respond to their environment with feelings of fear, disgust, anger, excitement, distress, delight, elation, affection, jealousy, and joy. As the child grows older these feelings continue to be exhibited toward persons and things outside the child and, eventually, when directed inward become the basis for the child's own self-concept.

In small children joy is experienced at its height when they are using their whole bodies, being totally involved in running, jumping, and shouting. This can be both the source of joy and the means of its expression. Or joy may come in response to a gift, to a projected favorite activity, or the sight of a friend or a returning parent. Even as children grow older, they feel joy primarily in relation to something pleasant that is happening to them, although because of their growing concept of time they are also able to experience joy as they anticipate future pleasurable events.

Only in older elementary years can children begin to experience joy in relation to abstract ideas. In a service of worship, when children carry banners they themselves have made, they may find joy in the experience of marching and feeling like a part of the total church community. The making of the banners can be an experience of joy because children are happy when they are making things, especially things that are seen to be of value. But only a few of the older boys and girls will derive joy from abstract phrases on banners. Joy for children is a "now" experience. For adults in this worship setting, the experience can be a celebration, a time to say, "See what God has done for me." For children, also, it can be a celebration: "See what I have done—I hope you like it."

The early fears of infancy will lessen as children reach the preschool years, although in certain circumstances, loud noises, sudden movements, or strangers can still elicit feelings of fear. In addition, new fears are being learned. Now children may be afraid of animals, the dark, imaginary creatures, being hurt, overly demanding social situations, or long separations from parents.

Through the course of the elementary years, children conquer these fears, one by one, as they begin to feel themselves in more control of their environment. Uncertain feelings caused by external circumstances become less significant and are replaced by uncertain feelings about themselves.

Children accept a great deal of love and attention and in return give indications of love, probably in order that the flow of love back to them will not be interrupted. This giving and receiving is the origin of feelings of trust, trust in the dependability of their world. And it is this ability to trust which is basic to later religious development. To paraphrase a familiar Bible verse, "How can you trust God, whom you have not seen, if you cannot trust your world of which you are a part?"

Children are equally capable of negative responses to others, feelings of mistrust, jealousy, and rivalry. For instance, jealousy may be directed toward children who seem to be winning more than their share of adult approval or toward an adult who is enjoying the desired attention of another adult. One preschooler became jealous of her father's doctoral dissertation which took time away from her and, as a result, attacked his typewriter!

As children grow toward adolescence they more and more express feelings of resentment toward adult control, even though the need for adult approval is still strong. In this struggle toward achieving their own identity they sometimes become moody, uncooperative, and even rebellious.

Whereas the emotions of younger children are largely produced by what the world does to them and for them, older children are beginning to respond with feelings about themselves and the way they relate to the world. In the elementary years, self-concept begins to be a more or less conscious developmental task for children. If their earlier years were relatively free from turmoil, they enter this period with a sense of self-assurance and with an eagerness to tackle whatever life brings. But these feelings are often accompanied by doubts and guilt as they slowly move away from dependence on parents and other significant adults. They have learned to discriminate between right and wrong, but sometimes they fail to act accordingly. When they make something and it meets their standards, they are pleased with themselves, but often they fall short of their own expectations. They want to be perfect, so they are easily discouraged. When they are accepted by the significant persons in their lives, whether adults or other children, they experience positive feelings of belonging; on other occasions they feel rejected and therefore undesirable.

So at times children feel good about themselves, at times they dislike themselves, and all the time they are creating a self-image.

But what if your parents weren't pleased to have you, so you never did learn to feel your world and the people in it were trustworthy? What if the kids at school call you bad names and you never feel good about yourself and nobody seems to care how you feel?

Mental Development

The Bible contains factual information and abstract concepts, so it is important to understand the mental development of children.

Acquiring and Verbalizing Ideas

By the time children are three years of age they have developed an extensive vocabulary and are beginning to construct sentences. Many of the sentences result from their growing curiosity and are in the form of questions: Why? Where? What for? and Who? Much of their speech is in imitation of adults in tone of voice, words, and ideas. One mother, upon meeting her child's kindergarten teacher exclaimed, "Now I know why Mary talks the way she does. She sounds just like you!"

When preschool children venture to express their ideas, they are not always able to discriminate between what has happened in the real world and what is a product of their imaginations.

The words and ideas expressed are related directly to their experiences, so children learn to verbalize most rapidly through participation in a variety of activities. They are more interested in the activity than in its potential for their learning, however.

Children in early elementary years are eager and curious about everything they see. They are beginning to have an interest in the past, especially if it is related to them personally in some way; for example, "This is where we lived when you were a little baby." Primarily, however, they are still oriented to the present. It is only in the later elementary years that children understand the concept of time—of past, present, and future. It is then that they can begin to understand history and make plans for future events.

Stages in Thinking

It is important to look more closely at the developmental process by which children change experiences into ideas and then learn to use those ideas to meet the demands of their world.

The first step in performing mental tasks is the ability to learn *concepts*. A child may be taught by rote to say, "The ball is round," but the concept *roundness* is not understood until the child is able to apply the word *round* to objects that are not spherical like the ball, but to objects such as wheels, saucers, and cylinders.

The second step in performing mental tasks is the ability to construct *principles*. Rolling and roundness are both concepts. Children show mental growth when they are able to combine the two concepts to form the principle: Round things roll.

The third and most complicated step in mental development is the ability to *combine principles* so as to form more complicated principles and to use these principles in order to solve problems. When the two principles "Round things roll" and "Friction decreases speed" are combined, a new principle about braking is discovered, and the problem of controlling speed is solved!

All the illustrations so far have dealt with concrete concepts, directly related to objects which can be manipulated. Round objects can be felt. Rolling can be observed. Friction can be applied. Braking can be tested, and the results measured.

Many concepts are not related to objects that can be manipulated. Love, force, faraway, before, spirit, and courage are just a few of the thousands of abstractions we use every day. These abstract concepts cannot be felt, moved, seen, or counted. It is obvious that it takes a higher order of mental development to understand the principle "love conquers force" than to understand "round things roll."

A Swiss psychologist, Jean Piaget, suggests that there are four major stages in the development of thinking, divided by age approximately into (1) birth to two years; (2) two to seven years; (3) seven to ten or eleven years, and (4) eleven years and over. Piaget asserts that children cannot begin to think in abstract terms until sometime during the third stage, and they cannot actually achieve abstract thinking that is useful and dependable until the last stage.

The Controversy

The controversy related to mental development usually is not centered around the sequence of steps or stages, but around the question of when a child is able to perform each mental task, at both the concrete and abstract levels, and how this may affect the teaching-learning process. Simply put, the argument is based on the answer to this question: What can children be expected to learn, and how early in their formal educational experience can they be expected to learn it?

As might be anticipated, there have been a variety of responses to this issue from educators whose task it is to make theories visible in classroom procedures. The responses fall into three general categories.

"We have underestimated children's ability to learn." Those who express this conviction point to the vast amount of materials children are able to memorize, their eagerness to learn as expressed through thoughtful questions, their fascination with educational television for children, the complicated manual tasks they can perform, and above all, their ability to read at an age far younger than the traditional six years. As a result of this point of view, many public schools have introduced reading in the kindergarten years.

Individualized instruction has been adopted to allow for the range of mental maturity in a given group of children. Where public schools have not adopted this approach, some parents have organized "free schools" or have supplemented the public school curriculum by teaching reading at home. Some have opted to remove their children from the "schooling" system entirely, and have joined the home school movement. Other parents have enrolled their children at the age of three in privately operated preschools which promise to teach reading and mathematics.

In the church school this understanding of the mental ability of children supports a general increase in the amount of content included in curriculum materials, especially the amount of Bible material. Most denominational curriculum revisions have been influenced by the assertion that "we have underestimated the ability of children to learn."

"Learning includes understanding." While agreeing generally with the premise that children's abilities have been underestimated, there are educators who insist that a word of caution be spoken. That is, the ability to pronounce words or to repeat concepts is not evidence that real learning has taken place. The important question to ask is, "Do the children understand what they have read?" Or, "Are they able to apply the concept in another situation?" Public school administrators and teachers who hold this view develop a readiness program to provide a basis on which a reading program can be built. The ability of children to distinguish shapes is determined before they are asked to see the difference between *b* and *p*. Care is taken to keep reading vocabulary within the experiences of the child. Where experience is lacking, it may be provided through planned activities. For example, a visit to the airport or a ride on a train may be made prior to reading a story involving various modes of transportation. The concern here is that an emphasis on reading skills is not made at the expense of comprehension.

Religious educators who join in the reminder that "learning includes understanding" point particularly to the abstract nature of important biblical concepts. "Pilots fly planes" is a principle capable of being grasped far earlier in the mental development of a child than the principle "God created the world."

"Growth in all areas of development is important." Some educators are anxious to raise a question about priorities and balance in education. Why is there such an emphasis in the early years on the area of mental growth? Children do not need to know how to read at three or four years of age. This can come later with no loss in future ability to learn. But children do need to achieve adequate emotional and social adjustment. If this is neglected in the

early years it will affect negatively their future development, including their ability to acquire reading skills.

A public school with this philosophy specializes in socialization in the kindergarten, saving the introduction of reading for the first grade. Throughout all the elementary years it will encourage teachers to set individual rather than group goals with the purpose of providing a balanced learning experience for each child. For example, a kindergarten girl who spends most of her time in the book corner will be encouraged to try the block corner for a few minutes each day, while a fifth grade boy who has interest in baseball only will be encouraged to join the school orchestra.

In church education this controversy is phrased in a somewhat different way: Why is there such concern that children be able to repeat theological concepts and doctrinal statements? Church education in the early years should develop attitudes about the Bible and the church.

Regardless of the way people respond to this present controversy in education, they all want to know more about the way children develop mentally at each stage so that they can work with this process.

But what if you are a slow learner or are gifted and bored or want to be a lawyer but your parents say, "Girls should be secretaries or nurses or mothers"? What if you are supposed to be learning about the Revolutionary War, but you really want to know how to protect yourself from the gang in the next block, or you move several times a year and you can't ever get caught up at school?

Religious Development

Finally we come to religious development only to discover that of all the areas the least research is here, the most inconclusive results, and perhaps the most overlapping with the other areas. Traditionally this research has been related to the development of religious concepts, and much of this has centered on the concept of God. There is no evidence in the studies available, however, that refutes Piaget's placement of abstract thinking in the later elementary years.

More recently the term "faith development" has come into being, due largely to the pioneer work of James Fowler (*Stages of Faith*, Harper & Row, San Francisco, 1981). Although often and erroneously used as a synonym for "religious development," faith development in Fowler's terms goes far beyond the acquisition of religious concepts. Faith, for Fowler, is the *way* a person finds meaning in life, not the set of religious concepts which may be articulated.

The Preschool Years

Jean McClarin Jones has described the preschool period as "the wonder years" ("The Religious Development of Children in Interrelationship with Identity Formation and Conceptual Growth," Boston University School of Theology, Th.D. diss., 1968). Here children attempt to find their identity as distinct objects in a world of many objects and, as a consequence, frequently ask of their parents many *how* and *why* questions. For the moment parents are seen as all-powerful because they have provided their children with all that they have needed. As the children's world expands they transfer this characteristic to other adults until, in imitation of adults, they at last assign to this all-powerful trait the word symbol *God*. Now there comes a flood of questions about God and the beginning of what we call "religious thinking."

The answers children receive to their religious questions are not intellectually understood by them because they still see God as a person like their mothers and fathers, even though the answers are given in terms of abstract concepts such as love, spirit, or divine. But there is evidence that children do exhibit a "sense" or "feeling" or "experience" of God. It is thought to be present in feelings of awe and wonder, such as those experienced when looking at a beautiful flower, really seeing a sunset for the first time, or watching a newborn baby. Adults explain these mysteries to the children by speaking the name *God*. Whether children eventually come to associate God with love and beauty or with punishment and deprivation depends on their experiences with their world.

Preschool children are fantasy-filled, with a power of imagination that is unencumbered by logic. Their faith life is strongly affected by the "visible faith" that they observe in the lives of the people who are most important to them. Fowler sees these two characteristics as basic in the faith development of preschool children.

Although children in the "wonder years" do not intellectually understand the concepts central to the Christian religion, they can begin to participate in its rituals because of their ability to imitate, and they can begin to use the name of God. Pleasure in this participation comes from the fulfillment of the social need to be a part of what significant adults see to be important and leads to the understanding of themselves as part of the church.

The Elementary Years

In contrast to the "wonder years" designation, children in the elementary grades are said to be in the "reality-oriented years." They are rooted in the here and now, and the here and now revolves around them as its center. God is one who does things to the child and for the child. Prayers by children in this period stress the personal benefits sought after. All in all, religion for children in the reality-oriented years must serve some useful function.

Elementary children ask more specific religious questions than the *how* and *why* queries of earlier years. Now they ask about birth, death, natural disasters, and God's role in all this. Whatever answers are given, whether in direct response or in formal instruction, they are always interpreted by children in terms of their own experiences. They may repeat the same words as those used by the adults, but their concept is never a precise copy of the adult's concept. Misunderstandings occur, therefore, and they tend to persist, leading to other misunderstandings.

As children approach the later elementary years they become more interested in the heritage of the church. They now begin to think abstractly, rather than having to identify each concept with some object in their experience. God no longer needs to be thought of in human form; love is a feeling, not a gift from grandmother, and sorrow is an emotion, not the tears themselves. It is only at this stage that children can begin to understand the doctrines of the church or begin to cautiously express their own faith statements.

Children in the late elementary years begin to find meaning as they tell the stories of their own experiences, and as they are able to enter into the stories of others, including the stories of their faith community. Fowler suggests that, for the moment, the meanings are "trapped" in the stories themselves; that the ability to step back from the story to discern meaning is not present until the early adolescent years. The meanings are more "felt" than "understood."

But what if your family never attends church and the only time you ever hear the word *God* is when someone is angry, or you drop out of Sunday school while you still visualize God as a man with a long white beard? Or what if nobody answers your questions, and if they do, you can't understand the answers?

Today's Child: A Stranger

In some ways, today's children are strangers. We have never been where they are. Although their world is changing, we know more about the world than we know about what it is doing to children. But the children are here today, and because we want to guide them in discovering Bible meanings now, we can do these things:

We can become careful observers of the child's world so that we can begin to see and feel how it is different from the one we knew when we were children.

We can use our creative imaginations to feel what it must be like to be a child today.

We can become familiar with those theories about childhood that have already been formulated, while continuing to be alert for new understandings as they become available.

We can avoid the temptation to generalize about children, determining to see each child as a unique individual, with his or her own personality and potential.

How is it possible for children in a rapidly changing world to be confronted by the Bible as an Event, in such a way that they discover in it meaning for their here-and-now lives? The next section describes what it means to teach biblically and how this point of view is supported by both the nature of the Bible and the nature of childhood.

6.
TEACHING CHILDREN BIBLICALLY

Since the beginning of this century there has been an ongoing debate among Christian educators—teachers, theorists, and curriculum writers. It has revolved around the question of whether teaching should be Bible-centered or life-centered. When asked the question, "What do you teach?" those who hold the first point of view reply, "I teach the Bible"; the second, "I teach children." Compromises have been attempted by offering some alternative centers from which to choose, but these always seem to fall into one camp or the other. At times the lines have been so tightly drawn by each side that any understanding of the other has been impossible. The fact of the matter is, there are some who are closer in thought to people in the other group than they are to some in their own.

The person who "teaches biblically" lives out in the classroom three basic convictions: (1) It is impossible to separate Bible and life, even should it be desirable to do so; (2) When life experiences are used as the basic materials, they must be interpreted within the context of the Christian community; (3) When Bible materials are used they must be taught experientially. These convictions are not necessarily stated by the teacher, but if they are really convictions, the Bible will come alive for the persons being taught.

Bible/Life—Inseparable

The distinction between Bible and life has been a false one from the beginning, and is a mind-set which should be eradicated. The fact is, the two are inseparable, for to say "Bible" is to say "Life."

The Bible itself verifies this unity in two ways. First, it shows itself in our understanding of the Bible as a written witness to Divine-human encounters. The Bible is not a set of propositions or creeds, but the testimonies of real people who experienced God in their lives. Without this "life dimension" the Bible would not exist.

Second, this unity of Bible and life is evident in our understanding of the Bible as a confronting Event to which we make a response. It is impossible for us to exist anywhere other than in our own life situation, so it is there that the Bible in its completeness confronts us. In this meeting the Bible and our life at that point are experienced as a single event. They are fused together in such a way that they cannot be separated.

If the Bible did not affirm this inseparableness, it would be affirmed by the nature of childhood. Whatever concepts children learn, they do it within the framework of their own experiences. Even if the life situations of children are never acknowledged by the teacher, children must struggle to find a way to fit what they learn about the Bible into their total concept of things.

"Teaching biblically" means not trying to separate Bible/life into two kinds of materials, but teaching in such a way that one will never be thought of without the other.

Christian Community as Context for Life-Experience Teaching

A teacher need not always deal with the Bible itself to be described as teaching biblically. Because the Bible is a witness to God's encounter with persons in their human situation, this is reason enough to consider life's experiences. While it is not always necessary to find answers to life's problems in specific Bible verses or to discover parallels in the lives of Bible persons, it is important that this examination of personal or social concerns be done within the context of the Christian community. Although this does not limit such teaching to an area within the four walls of the church, it surely means that it will be under the guidance of persons who acknowledge themselves to be within the Christian tradition and who function intentionally, at the request of and answerable to members of the Christian fellowship, usually the church. It also assumes that in previous sessions or units, biblical materials were taught and that this will be true in the future.

If early Christians struggled together to find meaning in their human situation, then it seems consistent with biblical tradition that life concerns today should be worked through with the help of the community of Christians. The church community can serve as a corrective for the interpretations, as a support for those who need encouragement, and as a reminder of our long heritage. It provides the rich resources of the tradition, many of them with their roots in the Bible—the sacraments, the liturgy, and the hymns of the church, for example.

To use today's concerns as materials for teaching, and to use them within the context of the Christian community, is part of what it means to teach biblically.

Teaching the Bible Experientially

Ever since the Christian community began, it has been convinced that when the Bible becomes real to persons, God is able to speak through it. We have called the Bible a "now" Event through which God confronts us and through which we find meaning for our lives. We want for our children what we want for ourselves. We want children to begin to develop a sense of being special persons who own a special tradition. We want them to begin to find heroes and heroines in the Judeo-Christian tradition as well as in secular history. We want to open the Bible to them so that God can use it to bring meaning to their lives, at whatever level and in whatever ways this is possible. We want children to know the Bible so that they can be confronted by it. We want the Bible to be an important part of the child's "now" world. And we want all of this to happen in their present, not in their future.

Is Present Meaning Possible?

But we cannot escape the question that has followed us since the close of the chapter, "A Confronting Event." Can the Bible be for children a confronting Event? There are three views, when seen in relation to one another, that support an affirmative answer to that question.

1. *The Bible is experience.* If the Bible is seen only as a collection of abstract religious concepts, and if to be Christian is to affirm these abstractions, it is useless to talk about the Bible and the religious life of children. We have already noted that children are unable to deal with such abstractions until at least the older elementary years. In effect, we would be following Goldman's proposal that in their early elementary years we help children get ready to be religious when they are ten or twelve years old.

But if we believe that the Bible and life cannot be separated, and we understand the Bible as a witness to how God has confronted and can continue to confront persons in their real-life situations, we realize that we are dealing not with a book of abstract concepts, but with reports of human experience. The Bible is a "living book" that speaks about the whole human situation and requires that we bring to the study of it all the abilities we possess, not just our ability to think abstractly.

2. *Children have experience.* Children do not come empty to their encounter with the Bible. They bring a vast reservoir of past experiences, so that when children meet the Bible, it is a meeting of experience with experience. As teachers better understand the development of children, and as they come to see the changing world through the eyes of children, they learn how to use the experiences that children bring to the teaching-learning process.

It should never be forgotten that part of the child's world is the presence in it of the Christian community. Although many factors affect religious development, the way children think, their emotional and social lives, and even their view of themselves is influenced by their identity as members of a particular religious community. And the past experiences with that community, along with all their other experiences, are the lenses through which they view all the events in their lives.

3. *Children can experience.* If what we have said about children is true, it is unreasonable to expect them to find and express meanings by the use of abstract thinking and wordings. However, it is not unreasonable to expect them to find and express meanings with the abilities they do possess. Rather than regret the absence of one kind of ability, we rejoice and build on the presence of others.

—*Children can feel emotions.* They feel joy, anger, fear, and loneliness, for example. They can feel a sense of belonging or a sense of awe and wonder. They can express their feelings through drama, art, dance, and music—and sometimes through words. When other people exhibit strong feelings, they often experience the same emotions. The many aspects of the problem of suffering unfolded in the story of Job cannot be intellectually understood, but children know how it feels to be judged in a way that seems unfair. They can know what it is like to have friends make fun of them for something they cannot help. They may not understand the cry of a nation, "O God, why does thou cast us off for ever?" (Psalm 74:1), but they can imagine what it would be like to come home alone to a locked and empty house.

—*Children are curious.* Once they get hold of a question, they will not let it go. They may not understand the theological differences in the two creation stories in Genesis, but they want to know how the world began. And they like to know that other people have asked the same question and found answers that satisfied them.

—*Children can manipulate things.* Through the use of elementary research tools and techniques, children are able to discover answers to some of their own questions. They can find answers on cassette tapes, in filmstrips, in dictionaries, in concordances, and in the Bible.

—*Children can identify with others.* They can identify with living persons and with persons in fiction and in history. In the important adults of the children's own lives they can see themselves when they are older. As they identify with these adults the children tend to take on the adults' values. By the time children are in kindergarten their circle of important persons has extended to include those beyond their immediate families so that church school teachers may become influences. When they do, teachers have an opportunity through their own attitudes to teach attitudes toward the Bible.

Those who guide children in the discovery of Bible meanings can build on all these abilities. In the intentional learning experiences provided by the Christian community, they can totally involve children by giving them opportunities to use all their senses, their bodies, their curiosities, their imaginations, their emotions, as well as their emerging abilities to think in abstract terms.

When children experience the Bible, they discover meaning in their own experiences because the Bible deals with human concerns. It speaks to the reality within each child, thus becoming a "now" Event.

Teaching for Future Meaning

Meaning for the present, as important as this is, cannot be the only consideration, because the child's future will be the youth's present.

In the childhood years it is not possible, or even desirable, to provide a complete Bible education. There are youth and adult years ahead in which meaning must continue to unfold. If the Bible is presented in the right way there will be no barriers erected in childhood that will tend to fix meaning at a child's level, limiting future under-standings. Nor will there be fostered the notion that "I've learned it all," so no further Bible study is necessary.

To teach for present meanings by building on the nature of the Bible as experience and the nature of the child as one who lives and grows in a sea of experi-ences—and to keep the Bible open for future interpreta-tions—is what it means to teach the Bible experientially, and therefore part of what it means to teach biblically.

Teaching experientially means finding ways to teach so that the Bible becomes as exciting an Event as yesterday's birthday party or tomorrow's space adventure. It means helping children experience the Bible as a living book that can become for them a confronting Event. Children taught in this way will feel with the Bible people rather than be told how they felt. They will find Bible persons with whom to identify. They will come to feel that the Bible is their book. And slowly but surely they will absorb the Judeo-Christian tradition and make it their own.

Experiencing Bible Content

The Bible does not become an Event for children if teachers attempt to transfer ideas from their minds to the minds of the children. Concepts arise out of experience. If children actually experience the Bible, it will be so vivid that it will become a part of their lives now. This does not mean that they will see Bible events as current history; it does mean that their association with the Bible will be a vital part of their real world. They will feel it, participate in it, handle it, own it. They will identify with the Bible characters. They will name their dogs and dolls Moses, Ezekiel, Mary, or Priscilla. They will hold imaginary conversations with Jesus or Paul or Abraham. They will turn the back yard or the alley or the barn into the temple, the stable, or Noah's ark. The Bible will not be something that belongs only to the past or the church or the teacher, but once they really experience it, it will belong to them—the children.

All the teaching methods known that can bring the Bible to life will be used. Since Bible stories will account for the greatest share of biblical materials used with children, the ability to tell stories will be important. But we will not depend on words alone.

We will use art to accompany the stories—the masterpieces, contemporary art, art from other countries. We will use music—the Psalms accompanied by children playing their rhythm instruments, hymns from the church's hymnal, children's songs, music to dance to. We will use drama—stories to pantomime, plays to read aloud, puppets through which to act, scripts to write and produce. We will use audio-visual materials as long as they are fast moving, dramatic, involving, and concerned with story line rather than facts. They can be projected pictures accompanied by a sound track or stories recorded on records or cassette tapes.

Sometimes we will plan activities that prepare children to enter into the spirit and feelings of the Bible story. Children can search the classroom for a well-hidden dime and then hear the story of the Lost Coin. They can paint a picture of how it feels to be lost—and found—and then hear the story of the Lost Sheep. They can be led through creative drama in an experience of what it is like to be hot and tired and lost in a desert and then hear the story of the Exodus. They can observe a baptism in the sanctuary and then hear the story of Jesus' baptism by John.

We will use some parts of the Bible that are not stories if they can be made real to children. Children can become familiar with the Ten Commandments, not as a moral code, but as part of a dramatic episode in the life of Moses. Children can use the Lord's Prayer, not as something to be learned by rote because it is there, but as a result of hearing it in worship experiences—beside their parents and other adults in the sanctuary and with their peers in the classroom.

There are some things we will not do. We will not suggest that retention of facts is the reason for telling Bible stories by requesting a playback of facts at the end of each story, or at the next session of the class. We will not append a moral to every story or wrap it up with "This means that" statements. We will not present Bible stories in a dull manner or imply they are dull by saying, "After we have had our Bible story then you can paste, color, or go outside and play—that is, have fun."

Only if Bible materials are presented so that they touch some respondent chord in the child will they have meaning.

Only if the Bible has meaning now will children look forward with expectation to the discovery of Bible meanings in the future.

Discovering and Expressing Bible Meanings

To say that Bible meanings are discovered is to say something special about the methods used to teach children the Bible. A uniquely shaped seashell, found after a search on a hot and windy beach and in the company of favorite people, is kept in a treasure box for a lifetime. A seashell dangling at the end of a key chain purchased at the discount store or given by a casual acquaintance is soon discarded.

The significant meanings that come as a result of the interaction of children with the Bible are not those transferred from teacher to child but those that surface as personal discoveries. They may or may not be the same ones found in the story by the teacher. But they belong to the child.

To speak of children discovering meanings in the Bible is not necessarily to speak of earthshaking insights that will forever change their lives. But it is to acknowledge that whenever children are really involved in an experience, they will attach importance to it. Their understanding may seem right, or it may be judged by us to be wrong, but in either case it is their understanding. It is a mistake to assume that the meanings discovered will be, or ought to be, crystal clear to the child. It is equally wrong to assume that every Bible passage has only one correct meaning. There are no final meanings. It is always possible to receive new insights, and good teaching keeps the doors open that will lead to further understanding.

7.
THREE GUIDELINES

It is difficult to imagine the time when the discovery of the common chalkboard was considered a great educational innovation! Perhaps this new method came in response to a generation of teachers who had pleaded, "Give us more ways to make our teaching effective." Today the problem is of a different kind. We often feel overwhelmed by the wide variety of teaching aids available to us. Each day brings announcements of new books containing "proven methods" or video tapes that promise to solve our problems. Many creative teaching methods are at hand, but it is difficult to know which ones to use and the proper time to use them.

The answer to effective instructional methods lies partially in issues addressed in the preceding chapters of this book: What is our understanding of children? What are they like? How do they learn? What are their abilities? What are their interests? What is our understanding of the Bible? What is its nature? What is its content? What is its significance for the Christian today? What results do we hope to achieve by teaching the Bible to children?

Finally, however, there is the teacher who insists on specific answers to specific questions: How do I help children want to know the Bible? How can I make the Bible more interesting? How can I tell if the children have found meaning in the Bible? On the basis of our understandings of both the Bible and children it is possible to address the "how to" questions of teachers.

As a result of both theoretical formulations and practical experience, three guidelines have emerged for teaching the Bible to children. The first guideline is a way to prepare children to hear the Bible story; the second is a response to the problem of making the Bible interesting; and the third focuses on Bible meanings.

Guideline One

The Bible is a written witness to the experiences of people in the past. It tells of weddings and funerals, feasts and famines. It is about wars between nations and rivalries between brothers and sisters. It portrays hikes on deserts and over mountains, musical instruments, and highway bandits. Through it all there is singing, dancing, praying, and weeping. And it affirms that in such experiences, people saw evidence of God's presence in the world.

Children are people, with an ability to understand things they can see, touch, taste, smell, and feel. Some of their concrete experiences are amazingly parallel to those of people in the Bible. At times children comprehend the events in their lives intellectually, but more often they understand with their emotions and imaginations.

But not all the experiences of modern children are found in the experiences of the Bible. It is a long way from space ships back to camel caravans, or from instantaneous news via satellites and television back to the era of the storyteller who traveled from village to village. A city child finds it difficult to understand the qualities of one described as being like a good shepherd, and even rural children today rarely watch yeast as it works its miracle in a loaf of bread.

Furthermore, even when the events of the Bible are similar to those of today, often the interpretations of those events as given by the biblical writers are beyond the understanding of children. They may appreciate the panic of the woman who frantically sought her lost coin, and even may understand why she would want to call in her neighbors for a celebration when it was found, but their world does not help them connect a found coin with "joy before the angels of God over one sinner who repents" (Luke 15:10).

One bridge between past and present is that people in both worlds share similar emotions. The feelings of joy and sadness, fear and confidence, and anger and love are universal. This is the common ground between the people of the Bible and today's children. Although shepherds and sheep may not be familiar, children can understand needing and receiving care.

The first guideline, then, in helping children experience the Bible, is to enable them to "feel into" the text. When they can feel the same emotions as those felt by the persons in the story, they are well on their way to understanding the story itself. "Feeling into" is similar to preparing the soil for the seed.

Any activity that can help children express emotion is a good "feeling into" activity. Especially useful are singing, dancing, painting, and creative drama. Less helpful is discussion, unless it is a sharing of feelings about experiences common to the children. The important thing to remember in choosing "feeling into" activities is that the emotions involved should resemble those in the Bible passage. Here are a few examples.

A Game

If children search until they find a well-hidden coin in the classroom, they will have felt both the frustration of searching for it and the joy of finding it. They can then easily enter into the spirit of the story of the lost coin, because they know how the woman felt.

Painting

If children paint to express how they feel when no one likes them, in the process they will bring to the surface feelings of loneliness, possibly the same as those Zacchaeus felt as he sat up in his tree. They will then be ready to "feel" along with Zacchaeus, as he marvels at the friendship offered by Jesus.

A Song

If children sing "The Runaway Song"[1] about a child who is assured of a parent's love, they will be able to appreciate the feelings of another runaway, the prodigal son, and his loving father.

Creative Drama

If children have a parade, marching to the strains of an imaginary band and waving imaginary placards, imagining that one of their heroes is present, they will be able to recapture the enthusiasm of the Palm Sunday crowds. They may even be able to feel the disappointment of the masses, when later Jesus turned out not to be the kind of political hero they were looking for.

Or, if through creative drama children can glimpse how it might feel to be captured as slaves, then promised freedom, only to be lost in a desert, and then miraculously saved, they will be able to hear the story of Moses and the Israelites as if it had happened to them.

Creative drama is one of the most effective "feeling into" activities because it utilizes all the ways people learn: the senses, the body, the imagination, the range of human emotions, and the mental abilities that have been developed. In the process, children experience real feelings.

Guideline Two

One of the tasks of childhood is learning about the adult world and finding appropriate ways to relate to it. The everyday occurrences in which children participate and through which they learn are part of that adult world.

[1]Mary Lu Walker, *Dandelions* (Paramus, N.J.: Paulist/Newman Press, 1975).

They learn acceptable eating habits by observing adults at the table. They learn about the nature of family life by living with a family. They learn to be "street-wise" from their experiences on the street. They learn there is a world beyond the home as they see their parents leave for work, as the family participates in community activities, and as they see older brothers and sisters leave for school. Because all these are observable and present experiences, it is comparatively easy for children to relate to them.

For those of us in the Christian community, the Bible is an important part of our adult world. But because it records past events in which children did not participate, they have more difficulty understanding it. However, even though it is difficult, the sharing of this tradition, by one generation with the next, is one of the ways religious development takes place.

Most children cannot comprehend the biblical text in even the most contemporary versions. Those who try are often discouraged and write off the Bible forever as an extremely dull, confusing book that has no meaning for them. The Bible needs a teacher, someone who can convey the traditional words so that they move with vitality out of the past into the child's present world. It needs a teacher who can make the events of the past so real that the Bible becomes an Event in the child's life.

The second guideline is to help children "meet with" the text in an exciting and involving way. The "meeting with" is the planting of the seed into the soil that has been prepared with "feeling into" activities. If the "feeling into" step has been a dynamic experience, the "meeting with" stage is simple. However, if it has been difficult to capture the emotions of the Bible passage in the first step, then "meeting with" must carry a larger share of the burden.

To "meet with" the Bible is much like receiving a snapshot on which is pictured a small segment of human experience. Some children may never have heard the story of the triumphal entry into Jerusalem, for example. You, as the teacher, have helped them "feel into" the story by having a parade for a present-day hero. The "meeting with" begins when you say, "When Jesus and his disciples came closer to Jerusalem, he said to them. . . ," and the "meeting with" ends as soon as the biblical narrative has concluded. When you began, the children had never heard the story, and when you are finished, they have heard it. They have "met with" the biblical text. For children who have heard the story before, the "meeting with" will be like seeing a snapshot of a familiar scene, but one that has been taken from a different point of view. In this step there is no introduction or discussion of the text—only the giving and receiving of the "snapshot."

The most appropriate methods for "meeting with" are those that are most likely to stimulate the child to say, "It feels as if I am really there!" Commercial sources have appreciated the difficulty of this part of the process and have flooded the market with cassette tapes, filmstrips, records, videos, flannelgraphs, puppets, and similar items. Many of these are excellent, especially when used along with "feeling into" and "responding out of" activities. Usually, however, they cannot stand alone and they never can substitute for a well-prepared teacher.

Here are some ways adults can help children "meet with" the content of the Bible.

Slides or Filmstrips

Slides and filmstrips are static media, so when these are used to tell a story, more attention must be given to the "feeling into" activities. The addition of a sound track increases their value in capturing the interest and imagination of children.

Video/Films

Dramatic, well-produced videos and films, which take into account the abilities of children to understand, can be almost as effective in making the Bible live, as if the children had been part of the actual event. The disadvantages of this form include cost, the availability of both resources and equipment, and the difficulty of finding films and videos that allow children to discover in the Bible story their own meanings.

Cassette Tapes, Records, and Compact Discs

Tapes, records, and discs that give a dramatic presentation of a Bible story can be more effective than filmstrips or slides, since they encourage the child's own imagination to create the pictures.

Songs

Music that tells the Bible story is inexpensive, and especially effective, because the song can be repeated many times without loss of interest. In fact, the more familiar a song becomes, the more it will be requested by the children. Melodies once learned return to mind again and again, and each time will remind the child of the words.

Reading Aloud

When it is anticipated that reading aloud from the Bible will provide the major "meeting with" experience, the reading must be extremely well done and accompanied by intense "feeling into" and "responding out of" activities. Reading may be used most effectively in connection with other "meeting with" activities. For example, after the children have learned and enjoyed the song "The Good Samaritan,"[2] the story of the good Samaritan then could be read from the Bible.

Storytelling

Storytelling is perhaps the best method for helping children "meet with" the Bible. It costs nothing, it is

[2]*Psalms and Songs* (Nashville: Graded Press, 1985), p. 41.

always available, and it helps children experience the way the Bible was handed down to us through oral tradition. Most of all, storytelling becomes a living symbol of the desire of one generation to pass on its tradition to the next. And when the story is finished, the storyteller is still there for the next phase of the Bible-teaching process.

Guideline Three

Children respond in some way to every experience in their lives. Sometimes they respond with words. Often they jump, run, clap, sing, or cry. At other times they may withdraw and seem not to respond at all, but even withdrawal is a definite response. Without some observable response, a teacher does not know what has been learned and consequently is not able to make plans for the next sequence of learning activities.

The writers of the Bible have recorded for us responses to experiences of divine presence. Moses' experience—God in a burning bush—was not the climax of that event, but only the beginning. God called for an action response from Moses when he declared, "I will send you to Pharaoh that you may bring forth my people, the sons of Israel, out of Egypt" (Exodus 3:10). Isaiah's vision of God concluded with a commitment response, "Here am I! Send me" (Isaiah 6:8b). After affirming the worth of persons by saying that we are like the salt of the earth and the light of the world, Jesus called on his hearers to respond with a quality of life: "Let your light so shine before men, that they may see your good works and give glory to your Father who is in heaven" (Matthew 5:16). When the rich man sought the way to eternal life, Jesus suggested that he sell what he had and give the money to the poor. He, too, responded: He went away sorrowful (Matthew 19:22).

The Bible as God's word is not only to be heard but also requires a response from us.

The third guideline, then, in helping children experience

the Bible is to encourage them to "respond out of" their encounter with the Bible text. This guideline is both biblically and theologically sound. If the Bible has been experienced through "feeling into" and an experiential "meeting with," a response of some kind will be inevitable. This response may be likened to the harvest that follows the planting of the seed in the prepared soil.

The teacher's task is to provide the classroom climate for a positive response. This may mean simply hearing and accepting the spontaneous comments or unspoken responses that come at the close of the story or other activity. It may mean making plans that will draw out or help children express what they feel but have not said. It will also suggest that you, as teacher or parent, share what the text means to you, since this exchange is an important part of teaching.

When children are asked to express their feelings and ideas, care should be taken that their comments not be manipulated so as to please the teacher. The suspicion that this often may happen has given rise to the unfortunate phrase "Sunday school answers." These kinds of answers are of no help to either the teacher or the child.

Not all responses will be directly related to the Bible itself. Some may be connected only vaguely: "That reminds me of once when we were in Colorado. . . ." Others may show reactions to the activity itself: "The man on the record who read the story had a funny voice!" Still another response may relate to the physical setting or to something that happened before the child left home. These do not fit naturally into the teacher's lesson plan, but they are valid responses for the children who make them, and need to be heard and acknowledged, even if only nonverbally.

There are four types of relevant responses that might follow "meeting with" a Bible passage: feeling, thinking, acting, and deciding.

Feeling Responses

After "meeting with" Psalm 100, children might feel like jumping for joy. Feelings about a "meeting with" the Lord's Prayer might be summarized through creative dance. After "meeting with" the rich young man who was called to decide how to live his life, the children might be ready to sing their feelings:

> Everywhere I turn, Something new to learn,
> But now at last I see, God made me strong and free.
> I'm the one finally who decides for me.[3]

Thinking Responses

Questions and answers and discussion are traditional ways in which we have led children to respond to Bible passages. Most prepared curriculum resources contain many examples of this kind of material.

Other possible thinking responses include creative writing of all kinds: litanies, plays, stories, newspaper accounts, scripts for slides or pictures, paraphrases of Bible selections, and words for songs. (Teachers sometimes assume that writing a Bible story in the form of a play, for example, is a "meeting-with" activity, but this is not so. To write a play, the children would have had to "meet with" the Bible story previously in some other way.)

Thinking need not always be an end in itself. When children are reluctant to express their feelings without words, a conversation might remind them of the feelings they had, and the session then might climax with a wordless feeling-response activity.

Acting and Deciding

Perhaps the most difficult form of response to the Bible is constructive action of some kind. For children, as well

[3]*Psalms and Songs* (Nashville: Graded Press, 1985), p. 89.

as for adults, it is usually easier to respond with words or with feelings. An extensive discussion of this aspect of "responding out of" will be found in Section Three, Chapter 10.

Bible teaching need not be a bore. But if it is to be a dynamic, life-renewing experience for children, it must treat the child as a whole person. The first step is to prepare the soil by helping the children feel the emotions inherent in the Bible story or passage to be taught. The second step is to plant the seed—to present the text as accurately and as effectively as possible, so the children will feel that they themselves were participants in the event. The third step is to reap the harvest by encouraging and accepting the children's responses to the Bible text.

8.
"FEELING INTO" THE BIBLE THROUGH CREATIVE DRAMA*

Creative drama is one of the most helpful and effective educational techniques to come from the theater. The primary reason that creative drama is so usable for the teacher who has no specialized training in theater is that it builds upon the child's natural interest in and ability to play. Anyone can use creative drama in the classroom. Be warned, however, that once teachers begin using creative drama, their interest often grows until they begin to buy books and take classes in order to learn more.

Creative drama is simply structured play that allows the child to participate physically, emotionally, intellectually, and imaginatively in a group experience of recollection. Anyone can take part because creative drama builds on two common human traits: the ability to experience and the ability to recall the feelings associated with experiences.

When introducing a Bible story to children, there are many advantages to using creative drama as a "feeling into" exercise. First, it involves the whole child—physically, emotionally, intellectually, and imaginatively—rather than only one aspect of the child. Second, it is a cooperative experience and cultivates the give and take of group interaction that subsequently helps children learn to respect the feelings of others. Third, it allows for active participation on the part of every player—every child can participate to the extent of his or her ability. Finally, by taking familiar feelings into new situations, each child enters a new learning environment through active involvement in the story.

*Written by Michael E. Williams.

Preparing to Use Creative Drama

All children are "experiencers" and can remember what it feels like to live through certain experiences. When we can remember the feelings we felt in one situation, we can re-create and apply these feelings in a new situation. In other words, creative drama helps us feel our way into the new situation. The new situation we are interested in "feeling into" here is a Bible story.

When we read or hear a story or see a movie, we naturally feel our way into the world of that story or movie. We usually do this by identifying with one of the characters. To identify with a character is as easy as saying, "I know what that feels like," or "I've felt that way." The moment we can say these things is the moment when we begin to experience the world of the story from the character's point of view.

Guiding Questions

The same process can be used to develop a "feeling into" exercise involving creative drama. When preparing to teach the story use these four questions:

1. Ask yourself these questions: "With which character do I identify and with which character or characters will the children most likely identify?" It is important to ask both questions because the children and adults are not necessarily drawn to the same character.

2. "What may this character be feeling?" The feelings that a character experiences in a story usually provide us an entry into the story and are the very reason we identify with the character.

3. "When have I felt that way?" Remember, feelings can be physical sensations such as hunger or thirst, or emotions such as happiness or sorrow. In what situations have you known such feelings?

4. "When might the children have felt the same way?" It is possible that your own remembered feeling was from childhood, but it is very important for the feeling to be one that the children will find familiar.

Tips to Remember

Other matters to remember as you begin to prepare a "feeling into" exercise are as follows:

Remember that this is *feeling* into, not *thinking* into. It is more productive to allow the children to recall the experience of joy in a group exercise than to say, "Think of a time when you were happy."

Remember that the "feeling into" always comes before the children hear the story. Of course, as teacher, you must be familiar with the story in order to create the exercise. Creative drama that occurs after the story would be "responding out of." Although creative drama is effective for this purpose as well, it is not the concern of this chapter.

Remember that the "feeling into" activity does not have to evoke the major feeling of the story, but a feeling that will get the children into the story.

Remember that if the dominant feelings in the story are unfamiliar to most children or are ones that might be too frightening or harmful, you may choose not to use that story. Some stories, such as Abraham's near sacrifice of Isaac, might well be saved for a later age.

Remember, "feeling into" is not group therapy. The purpose here is to provide an experiential entrance to the Bible story.

Finally, remember never to exploit the feelings of the children in a destructive way. For example, never select a group (such as, blue-eyed or left-handed children) to receive special favors or to be excluded. Although this might help them to better understand prejudice, it is a method that is negative and exploitative.

You are now ready to plan for a creative drama experience through which children, by the power of their imaginations, will be able to identify with the feelings of Bible people, and thus "feel into the story itself." The story of "Joseph and His Brothers" is used to illustrate how this is done. Before going on familiarize yourself with the story by reading Genesis 37:4-36.

"Joseph and His Brothers": The Guiding Questions

Begin by recalling the four questions listed earlier.

1. With whom do you identify?

Among the characters in the story are three with which any reader is most likely to identify: Jacob, Joseph, or the brothers.

2. What may these characters be feeling in the story?

In this story, here are some of the specific feelings that may be associated with each character.

Jacob
love for his wife and son
grief at the loss of his son

Joseph
feeling of being special
feeling of being trapped in the pit
relief in being rescued, only to face the unknown

Brothers
feeling of being left out of father's love
jealousy and vengefulness toward Joseph
regret at their father's grief

3. When have you felt this way?

Choose one of the feelings of one of the characters and try to remember a situation in which you felt as he did. If you are having difficulty, pick another character or feeling. It is important that the teacher be able to experience with some vividness the feeling that the children are being asked to recall.

Jacob
Whom have I loved the way Jacob loved his wife and
son?
When have I felt grief like Jacob's at his son's loss?

Joseph
When have I felt special?
When have I felt trapped?
When have I been rescued only to face the unknown?

Brothers
When have I felt left out?
When have I felt jealous or vengeful toward someone?
When have I regretted something I did because it hurt
another?

4. When have the children felt this way?
There are certain feelings that adults have experienced
which are outside the realm of a child's understanding.
There also are feelings that might prove destructive or
frightening to the child. Both of these must be avoided. If
you cannot remember an experience from your childhood
that is readily associated with one of the feelings you have
chosen, ask a child. "Tell me about a time when you felt
special" or "Tell me about a time when you felt left out."

Jacob
Toward whom have the children felt love?
When have the children experienced the grief of loss?

Joseph
When have the children felt special?
When have the children felt trapped?
When have the children been rescued from a situation
to face an unknown future?

Brothers
When have the children felt left out?
When have the children felt jealous or vengeful?
When have the children felt regret because something
they did hurt another?

"Joseph and His Brothers": Some "Feeling Into" Activities

Now you are ready to develop the "feeling into" activity that will allow the children to enter into the story of Joseph and his brothers. Following are several suggested activities based upon the feelings of the characters in the story. They were developed in response to the guiding questions discussed earlier. Although a number of activities are presented, you need to develop only one for each story. Those following suggest some of the variety of "feeling into" activities that can come from the same story. You may wish to adapt these or develop your own.

"Feeling Into" Activity Based on Jacob's Feelings

Choose an animal that most of the children would recognize as a pet (a dog or cat). Ask the children what it sounds like, and let the children make the sound. Ask the children what it looks like when it walks, and let them imitate its movement. Now ask how much the pet weighs and how big it is. Let the children demonstrate how they would pick it up if it were their pet. Then ask the children to show the pet how much they love it. Would they pet it or hold it or feed it? Ask the children to put their pets down and to gather around. Call for your own pet and ask the children to call for theirs. Say, "Our pets must have wandered away. Let's look for them." Ask the children to look for their lost pets as if they were really missing them. How would they call for their pets and how would they look for them? Ask the children to remember how it feels to lose their pets. Then say, "Here they are." Suggest that the children pick up their pets and greet them so that the pets know how much the children missed them.

Now you are ready to let the children "meet with" the story of a father's grief at the loss of his son.

"Feeling Into" Activities Based on Joseph's Feelings

Give each child a special imaginary gift unlike anyone else's in the room. Be sure to explain that this gift is like no other and gives the child special abilities or privileges. For example, one child can stay up as late as she wants, another can watch whatever he wants on television, while another has to eat only the foods she likes. Perhaps one child can be invisible any time he wants, or another can make any kind of food taste like ice cream. Be sure to plan a special gift for each child. Ask the children to tell one another about their special gifts and to explain how the gifts make them feel. You may want to whisper to each child what his or her gift is, or wrap up small packages with the gift described on slips of paper inside. Now you are ready to tell the story of Joseph, who was pampered and who lorded it over his brothers.

Ask each child to name his or her favorite animals that they have seen at the zoo or on television. Instruct the children to become their favorite animals and to make the animals' sounds. Now, tell the "animals" that each of them is in a cage. They can move around within their cages, but they cannot touch one another. Let the children move in their cages as the animals would. Remind them that they cannot leave their cages or touch another animal. Now, the zookeeper (you) walks through the zoo and closes the imaginary curtains surrounding the cages so that each animal is in the dark. How does each animal feel? What sound would the animal make trapped inside the dark cage? After they have made their animal noises, let the children out of their cages so that they may hear the story of Joseph in the pit.

Divide the children into pairs, or ask each child to choose a partner. Ask one of each pair to close her eyes while the other leads her around the room and describes the scenery of a land to which she has never been. Scenery might include trees, mountains, or rivers. The partner can lead the other child over obstacles such as logs, rocks, and streams. The partner may describe but never tell where he is taking the other child. After a few minutes, ask the partners to switch roles. Then ask the children to sit and to hear how Joseph faced an unknown future in a foreign land.

"Feeling Into" Activities Based on the Brothers' Feelings

Ask the children to find comfortable places to sit, separated from one another, and to close their eyes. Then ask them to imagine that they are all alone and that they can hear children playing somewhere in the distance but cannot join them. How do they feel? To make things worse, their families went on vacation but left them home with a babysitter. How do they feel? What's more, their best friend got a bicycle for Christmas (substitute any popular or desirable toy), but they did not. How do they feel? Now ask the children to gather and to hear a story about a group of brothers who felt left out.

You, as teacher, are in a very elite club consisting of one member. Create a clubhouse out of found materials (old cardboard boxes, pieces of cloth, and such). Ask the children if they would like to join your club. Each child must give you a good reason that you should let him or her be a member. For every reason offered, you offer a reason that he or she cannot be a member. The reasons do not have to make sense, since this sort of exclusiveness never does. Your reason may be that the sky is blue or that you had cereal for breakfast this morning. Do not choose a reason that may be hurtful or destructive to a child, and do not pick an attribute that may single out a child (blue eyes or left-handedness, for example). Since you will not let anyone else join your club, suggest that the children talk about how your behavior makes them feel and what they are going to do about it. (Will they form their own club, for instance?) Then ask them to sit and to listen to a story about a group of brothers who were jealous of their brother.

Next Steps

Now you are ready to begin. Creative drama not only helps children feel their way into Bible stories, but it also makes the stories more fun for the children and the teacher alike. It allows us to become children again and to see the Bible stories with new freshness. Anyone can take part. All you need is a few collected materials such as scraps of cloth, boxes, wooden blocks of various shapes and sizes, and an imagination. Every child (and every teacher) has the power of imagination.

Using creative drama allows a child to participate as fully as possible in the stories of the Bible. It helps children get in touch with their own feelings and the feelings of others. Creative drama calls upon all of children's resources as human beings: to feel, to think, and to imagine. Finally, it introduces children to the characters of the Bible as flesh and blood human beings who have feelings just as they do. Bible characters are no longer pictures in a book or cartoons on a screen, but they take on flesh and become a part of each child's life. This, after all, is why we tell the stories in the first place. Now you are ready to "meet with" these characters through storytelling.

9.
"MEETING WITH" THE BIBLE THROUGH STORYTELLING*

Storytelling is one of the most ancient customs of the human race. For untold centuries people have gathered as families and in larger groups to share their experiences, dreams, and fantasies in stories. Some of those tales belonged to the entire community and were told again and again. As children in communities listened to storytellers, they began to know and experience the traditions of their people.

The Bible is a reservoir of such stories and images that all Christians share, and many are shared with members of the Jewish community, as well, through the Old Testament. Many were passed down from generation to generation long before they were ever recorded in written form. Even though our interpretations of these stories may differ, we are united by this common heritage.

The Value of Storytelling

Through storytelling, four areas of human experience are enriched for both the tellers and the hearers: (1) imagination; (2) relationships; (3) feelings; and (4) response.

Imagination

Imagination is a human being's ability to experience events, persons, and things that are not physically present. We experience the events that take place in our imagination with all our senses. It is the place of memories, dreams, and fantasies. Sometimes people have viewed the imagination with disfavor, saying, "That's just your imagination." Recently psychologists

---

* Written by Michael E. Williams.

and philosophers have begun to discover the truth that poets, artists, and storytellers have known for centuries: what we remember of the past and what we hope for in the future depend upon our ability to participate in the sights and sounds of our imaginations.

Pictures, books, slides, films, videos, and television provide ready-made images, but storytelling encourages both those who tell and those who listen to exercise their imaginations by creating their own images. Through imagination, children are able to transport themselves to other places and other times, and in this way they can begin to enter into the experiences of persons who lived long ago in Bible times.

Relationships

There are three primary relationships involved in any storytelling experience. First, we come to know the story in the person of the storyteller. Through the teller's words, the story world is created and presented to those gathered to listen. In that moment the story exists in the relationship between the teller and the hearers.

Second, as the story is told, we come to know and care about the persons who inhabit that story world. The characters of the story then become a part of our experience that is carried into our daily lives.

Third, storytelling is a public act. A story does not live until it is shared. Those who have experienced the story together become a community created by the story world they have shared. Therefore, as tellers and as hearers, we can find a relationship to the church community by the stories we have told and heard there.

Storytelling is an especially appropriate way to help children "meet with" the Bible because it is an experience through which children can come to know and care about the teller, the persons in the story, and the community that shares the story.

Feelings

As we listen to stories, the characters and events of each story come to us not as themes or meanings but as persons and events. Stories may excite, anger, soothe, or confuse us, but when they are told well, we are touched by the world they create. Some stories can transform our lives and radically change the way we view the world. Many of the parables told by Jesus often overturn what we have been taught to expect. It must have startled his listeners when Jesus told a story in which an outcast Samaritan showed greater compassion than did the accepted religious leaders.

Response

Finally, stories provide an experience to which persons can respond. The response may take the form of another story, a dance, a painting, or a poem. Each time a story is told, it becomes a new Event. Each time the story is heard, we discover a new delight and depth, which in turn open unexplored possibilities for response out of the experience.

Preparing to Tell a Story

Few of us feel confident as storytellers, especially as tellers of Bible stories. When the church school teacher's guidebook suggests that we tell a story from Scripture, most of us resort to reading the text directly from the Bible or from a Bible storybook. This is not necessary, because storytelling is not that difficult. Here some ways to prepare and present Bible stories are suggested. These methods require no special training beyond an interest in becoming a better storyteller and a willingness to invest the time and effort required to prepare the story well.

The process involves three stages: (1) choosing the story; (2) getting to know the story; and (3) practicing the story.

Choosing the Story

Church school instructional materials usually suggest the Bible selection most appropriate for the session. In these cases, the choice has been made for you, and you can proceed to prepare the story for telling. If, however, you find yourself in charge of a class, an informal gathering of children, or an intergenerational event for which there is no prescribed lesson plan, or if you are a parent who wishes to tell stories at home, you must first choose a story. Often the first choice is a story that is a favorite of yours. Though this is a natural tendency, this method of choice severely limits the possibilities.

The four areas of human experience enriched by storytelling can serve as guides. Begin by asking yourself (the teller) questions about the story, relating these areas. Does the story spark my *imagination*? Are the characters in the story significant enough to make a *relationship* with them important? Does the *feeling* of the story move me deeply, make me laugh, cry, think? Is it rich enough in characters and action that I could hear it again and again, *responding* to different aspects of the story each time? The more often you are able to answer yes to these questions, the better you will be able to tell the story so that it will have meaning for your listeners.

The next step is to ask certain questions about the relationship of the story to those who will hear it. Will the story exercise the *imaginations* of children, even if its images are understood concretely? Are the characters of the story valuable additions to the community of persons and characters with whom the child is already in *relationship*? Does the story have *feelings* within it with which the children can identify? Will the story encourage a variety of creative *responses*? Yes answers to these questions indicate that the story has a potential for providing a meaningful experience for both the teller and the listeners.

Getting to Know the Story

Storytellers need to be freed from the idea that a story must be memorized. In fact, memorization can stand in the way of good telling. A memorized story is always in someone else's words, rather than your own. A story that is memorized is not flexible enough to allow for elaboration or simplification as the situation demands. If children interrupt in the middle of a story with a question or comment on the action, memorization does not allow you to respond without shattering the world created by the story.

If you are not going to memorize a story, you will need another way to recall it so that you can tell it with confidence. Some very short stories may be remembered simply by going over the events until their order is learned. There is another method useful for learning longer, more complex stories. This technique is called scoring, and is an adaptation of a design by Barbara McDermitt of the School of Speech at Northwestern University.[1]

A score for a story is much like the score for a piece of music. In a story score, instead of notes, there are word clues for the teller. Both scores are divided into units of action; in music, these units are called measures, but in a story score, they are called scenes. When the setting

	PLACE	CHARACTERS	OBJECTS	ACTIONS
Scene 1.				
Scene 2.				
Scene 3.				

[1]Adapted from a chart designed by Leland H. Roloff, Department of the School of Speech, Northwestern University, for the scoring and analysis of fairy tales, and used in the class "Literature and Body Thinking."

changes, or when a new character appears, the story moves to a new scene. Finally, both musical and story scores always use the same general format. Rather than being a musical "staff," the story format is a grid that looks like the one on page 96.

The story of the feeding of the five thousand can be used to show how a story score is created. Since there are four versions of this event in the Gospels, you are faced with the necessity of choosing a source for your story (Matthew 14:13-21; Mark 6:30-44; Luke 9:10-17; John 6:1-15). You can choose the story as told in one of the Gospels, including only the details found there, or you can combine the elements from two or more of the Gospels to create your own version of the story. You, as teller, are free to use your knowledge of Bible backgrounds to expand on the description of characters and events so that the listeners may experience the world of the story more fully.

Now you are ready to work through the story scene by scene. For the purpose of this illustration, materials were drawn from all four Gospel accounts.

In scene 1, Jesus hears of the death of John and tells the disciples he wants to get away from the crowd and be alone.

	PLACE	CHARACTERS	OBJECTS	ACTIONS
Scene 1.	crowded city	Jesus & disciples John crowd		hears of John's death; goes to be alone

Scene 2—the boat trip of Jesus and the disciples on the Sea of Galilee to a place near Bethsaida. Here the change of location signals a different scene.

	PLACE	CHARACTERS	OBJECTS	ACTIONS
Scene 2.	Sea of Galilee	Jesus & disciples	boat	sails to Bethsaida

Scene 3 takes us back to the crowd Jesus left, who, hearing where he is going, follow along a land route by foot, by donkey, cart, and wagon, in order to arrive at Bethsaida ahead of him. A change of both character and location indicates a change of scene here.

	PLACE	CHARACTERS	OBJECTS	ACTIONS
Scene 3.	crowded city	crowd	feet donkeys carts wagons	crowd follows Jesus

In scene 4, Jesus and his disciples bring the boat to shore near Bethsaida, only to find the crowd already waiting.

	PLACE	CHARACTERS	OBJECTS	ACTIONS
Scene 4.	country- side near Bethsaida	Jesus & disciples crowd	boat shore	Jesus lands, crowd is waiting

In scene 5, Jesus has compassion on the crowds of people and begins to teach and heal them in spite of his own grief.

	PLACE	CHARACTERS	OBJECTS	ACTIONS
Scene 5.	country-side near Bethsaida	Jesus crowd		Jesus has compas-sion; teaches and heals

Scene 6 begins on the evening of the same day. Note that a time change signals a scene change here. The disciples suggest that Jesus send the crowd to the city to find food.

	PLACE	CHARACTERS	OBJECTS	ACTIONS
Scene 6.	country-side near Bethsaida	Jesus & disciples crowd	food	disciples want to send crowd away

In scene 7, Jesus tells the disciples to feed the crowd from the food they brought with them. The disciples reply that they have only five loaves of bread and two fish. John's Gospel says this food is offered by a child.

	PLACE	CHARACTERS	OBJECTS	ACTIONS
Scene 7.	country-side near Bethsaida —evening	Jesus & disciples crowd	5 loaves 2 fish	Jesus tells disciples to feed crowd

In scene 8, the crowd is seated in smaller groups. Jesus blesses the loaves and the fish and tells his disciples to pass the food among the crowd.

	PLACE	CHARACTERS	OBJECTS	ACTIONS
Scene 8.	country-side near Bethsaida —evening	Jesus & disciples crowd	5 loaves 2 fish	crowd sits in groups; Jesus blesses food; disciples distribute food

During scene 9, the crowd eats its fill and there are twelve basketsful left over. And the story says there were over five thousand people gathered there.

	PLACE	CHARACTERS	OBJECTS	ACTIONS
Scene 9.	country-side near Bethsaida —evening	over 5,000 people	12 bas-ketsful leftover pieces	crowd eats fill

Having completed the scoring process, the finished score would look like this:

	PLACE	CHARACTERS	OBJECTS	ACTIONS
Scene 1.	crowded city	Jesus & disciples John crowd		hears of John's death; goes to be alone

Scene 2.	Sea of Galilee	Jesus & disciples	boat	sails to Bethsaida
Scene 3.	crowded city	crowd	feet donkeys carts wagons	crowd follows Jesus
Scene 4.	country-side near Bethsaida	Jesus & disciples crowd	boat shore	Jesus lands, crowd is waiting
Scene 5.	"	Jesus crowd		Jesus has compassion; teaches and heals
Scene 6.	" —evening	Jesus & disciples crowd	food	disciples want to send crowd away
Scene 7.	"	"	5 loaves 2 fish	Jesus tells disciples to feed crowd
Scene 8.	country-side near Bethsaida —evening	Jesus & disciples crowd	5 loaves 2 fish	crowd sits in groups; Jesus blesses food; disciples distribute food
Scene 9.	"	over 5,000 people	12 basketsful leftover pieces	crowd eats fill

After you have created and used a score, you will want to keep it to refresh your memory when you have occasion to tell the story again at some future time.

Practicing the Story

Before the story is told in public, it should be practiced aloud several times for one or more persons, preferably near the age of your anticipated audience. Tell the story as often as you can, for the more often you tell it, the sooner it will become your own.

The score provides only the skeleton of the story. As it is practiced you will elaborate by adding details to create the sights, sounds, odors, and other sensory experiences of the world in which the story takes place. In the feeding of the five thousand, the soft rhythmic splashing of the sea, the creaking of the boat, and the aroma of the bread and fish can excite the imagination. However, it is important that the addition of detail does not stop the flow of the story's action. This is especially crucial with young children, because it is the action that holds their attention.

Telling the Story

At last comes the day you have been preparing for. It is time to tell the story. You will need to be aware of several things.

The Room

Are the listeners facing away from a door or window that might otherwise prove distracting? Are you sitting where you can be seen by all? Are the listeners sitting so that you can maintain eye contact, even with those on the outer edge of the group?

The Age of Your Audience

Different aspects of a story will appeal to different age groups. While action may hold the attention of younger children, the characters in the story may attract older ones. Even if the story is suitable for the age of your listeners, you will hold their interest more closely by directing it to their level of experience.

The Attention of Your Listeners

It is natural for attention to drift, because it is hard for children to concentrate for long periods, even if they are interested in the story. Because this is especially true of younger children, it is advisable to keep the telling time for their stories to a minimum. In a longer story, watch to see if your listeners are maintaining eye contact with you or if some, especially at the outer edge of the group, are beginning to grow restless. If you are aware of these signs, you will be able to pull their attention back for the high points of the story. Remember these tips: maintain eye contact with as many people in the group as possible; let each person feel that you are telling the story to him or her.

Flexibility

If a child asks a question or makes a comment in the middle of a story, attempt to respond without breaking the flow of the story. For example, if a child asks practical questions about how long it took to get to Bethsaida or why the disciples brought so little food, the answer may be vague ("Oh, it took a long time"), or more specific ("Well, they didn't expect to have to feed all those people!"). Although questions should not be encouraged during the telling itself, when they do occur, it is important to acknowledge them.

The Ultimate Fear

What if I forget?
Try not to be upset, because it has happened to the best of storytellers. It is always appropriate to ask, "Now where was I?" or "Who was I talking about?" Not only does this keep the story moving, but it acknowledges that the listeners are participants in the storytelling event.

Discover your own style. One teller may have a flair for the dramatic, while another has a fairly matter-of-fact style, and still another is a quiet teller. Each can create the world of the story and touch the listener with its characters and events. The important thing is that your style of telling should be appropriate to the story, to your audience, and to you as a person. The best advice is to prepare thoroughly, relax, and enjoy the telling. In this way, children can meet with the Bible persons and events, as they hear the ancient voices and imagine the ancient faces of such people as Abraham, Ruth, Joseph, the prophets, and Jesus. Through your telling, they will come to know the stories shared by Christians in all ages and places.

10.
"RESPONDING OUT OF" THE BIBLE WITH DANCE, DIALOGUE, AND DEED

When children are helped to "feel into" the Bible text, and when they meet with the text in an experiential way, the parent or teacher can expect that they will be able to respond to this experience of the Bible. Sometimes the response will be spontaneous. At other times adults will plan activities that will encourage response. This chapter describes only three possible forms of response: *dance,* or creative movement; *dialogue,* and interactive and depth style of conversation; and *deed,* an action and service-centered response.

DANCE*

Moving one's body rhythmically in order to show emotion has been a natural means of expression for thousands of years. The Bible records that the early Hebrews danced to show their feelings of joy and sorrow, praise and pain. In II Samuel 6:14, it is recorded that when the ark was brought to Jerusalem, "David danced before the Lord with all his might." In Psalm 149:1-3, the people are admonished to "sing to the Lord a new song . . . praise his name with dancing," and in Psalm 150:3-6, we find:

> Praise him with trumpet sound;
>   praise him with lute and harp!
> Praise him with timbrel and dance;
>   praise him with strings and pipe!
> Praise him with sounding cymbals;
>   praise him with loud clashing cymbals!
> Let everything that breathes praise the Lord!
>   Praise the Lord!

* Written in collaboration with Carol Johnson Sorenson.

With skillful and sensitive guidance, dance is an appropriate way to respond to encounters with the biblical text. Because it allows children to use their bodies, their feelings, and their imaginations, as well as their minds, it can help them express meanings that would be impossible with words alone. The more intense the "feeling into" activity has been, the more free and able children will be to "respond out of" the Bible text in creative ways. (In this chapter, we are using dance for a particular purpose—response; it also can be used for "feeling into," in much the same way as creative drama, described in chapter 8.)

Before you use dance with children, you will need to do three basic things: (1) carefully introduce them to dance as a method of learning and expression; (2) be sure that dance is an appropriate way to respond to the Bible text at hand; and (3) develop a teaching plan.

Introducing Children to the Idea of Dance

Children are natural dancers! Watch small children when they hear music. Unless restrained by adults or lack of space, their bodies will instinctively move in rhythm with the beat. They clap, skip, jump, stretch, twirl, stand on tiptoe and fall to the ground. Unfortunately, by the time children reach elementary school, they have learned that such spontaneity is not an acceptable form of behavior, so when indoors and in the presence of adults, they limit their impulses to wiggling, and finally to politely "sitting still." Nevertheless, when out-of-doors and free from restrictions, they return to expressive and exuberant movement.

Since the church school setting is both inside the building and supervised by adults, some of the learned restraints will need to be removed before children will feel free to use their bodies in an expressive way. You may need to work on this for several weeks before you plan to have your first experience with dance as a response.

When to Introduce the Idea

When introducing the idea of dance to children, you may be able to take advantage of various church school settings. If you plan to use it in a church school session, you might begin your introduction four to six weeks ahead of time by scheduling five minutes at each session. Or, vacation church school will allow more time, perhaps twenty to thirty minutes, for introduction activities. Another possibility would be to use larger blocks of time during the Sunday school hour for one or two weeks. But whatever you do, you will need to consider your individual class and how the preparation time will fit into the purpose of the unit you are teaching.

How to Introduce the Idea

There are many ways to help children feel free to express themselves through creative movement. Some time before you plan to use dance as a way to respond to the Bible text, try some of these activities.

1. **Follow-the-leader.** Children line up as if to play the usual game of follow-the-leader. Ask the leader to concentrate on moving just one or two parts of the body—for example, just head and elbows. All the other children will try to follow, using as much of the available space as possible, and trying to make the movements flow smoothly through the space. After a minute or so, choose another leader, and focus on other parts of the body, perhaps this time the knees and fingers.

2. **Imaginary Baseball.** Have children take positions for a game of imaginary baseball. As they play, encourage them to make the movements as big and flowing as they possibly can. They can create a whole series of dance movements, one for each position on the team. This

activity is well received by girls and boys who enjoy sports.

3. **Balloons in the Air, Always.** Divide the class into groups of four, providing two balloons for each group. The purpose of the game is to keep the balloons in the air as long as possible by batting them with various parts of the body. This can also be done as one large group.

These first three activities focus on freeing children to use all parts of their bodies. The next three are concerned with helping children not only to move without inhibition, but also to express specific emotions through movement.

4. **"-ing" and "-ly" Words.** Make two sets of flash cards: one set with "-ing" words such as running, jumping, skipping, falling, hopping, and walking; a second set with "-ly" words such as happily, sadly, angrily, lightly, energetically, and timidly. Choose two words, one from each set, call them out to the class, and let the children dance their interpretation.

5. **Mood Music.** Choose a piece of music with an obvious mood, such as "joy." Ask the children to show by the way they move how the music makes them feel. Play "sad" music as a contrast and once again ask them to show how they feel. Later they will be ready to interpret music that portrays more subtle and varied moods.

6. **Crepe Paper.** Give children long scarves or streamers of crepe paper as a variation when using mood music or "-ing" and "-ly" words. Props such as these help children feel less inhibited, since they can give their attention to the object and not to themselves.

When children have caught the idea that "inside feelings" can be expressed by "outside body movement," they are ready to respond to biblical passages through dance.

Development of a Teaching Plan

The teaching plan is the third major task in helping children "respond out of" the Bible through dance. The planning process can be divided into four steps: (1) warm-ups as "feeling into" activities; (2) "meeting with" the Bible passage; (3) dance as a response; (4) concluding the session.

Warm-Ups as "Feeling Into" Activities

The "feeling into" activity is an ideal time to involve children in warm-ups. Bodies and imaginations can be limbered up at the same time. For example, children may be asked to imagine that they are having a snowball fight; some are throwers and others are targets. Targets are not allowed to run away, but must stay in one place. After a few minutes, children may change roles. Then the story of Stephen may be told—a man who, instead of snowballs, had stones thrown at him, and whose only crime was that he was a Christian.

Or, children may be asked to imagine they are in jail, tied so that they are unable to move. When they awake from sleep they discover that mice have chewed through their ropes, and they are free! They rub their wrists and ankles, stretch to hasten the return of circulation to their numbed bodies, and finally try to find a way out of the prison. This can be followed by the story of Paul, who was freed from prison chains by an earthquake. In both instances, the warm-up activities that encourage free body movement also call for the emotions that will add significance when the stories are heard.

"Meeting with" the Bible Passage

The Bible text may be presented in any of the ways described in chapter 7. Perhaps the most simple and effective way would be through storytelling.

Dance as a Response

Now that the children have "felt into" the story and "met with" it, they are ready to be encouraged to move freely and creatively in response to those feelings. There are four steps the children can be led to follow naturally as they express their feelings through dance.[1]

1. Grasp the idea with the imagination. Children have been helped to do this through the warm-up activities and the telling of the story.

2. Play Statues. Ask the children to show with a stationary body posture how the story has made them feel, or how they think some person in the story may have felt. For example, "Become a statue and show me how you imagine Stephen looked and felt when the people to whom he preached threw stones at him." Or, "Become a statue and show me how you felt when you heard that Paul and the other prisoners did not try to escape."

3. Move in place. Now, let the children move and twist their bodies without leaving their places, in order to show even more how they or the person in the story felt. Encourage them to extend their bodies in all directions, making the "statue" bigger, or to contract their bodies, making the "statue" smaller. Bigger and smaller, bigger and smaller, always moving smoothly from one size to the other, and always keeping the feelings they seek to portray vividly in their imaginations.

4. Move to another place. Children are now ready to move to other spots in the room, repeating these actions. Encourage them to change their locations slowly and with flowing motions, so as not to interrupt the rhythms they have established. As they reach their new places, they may want to express different emotions. A background of appropriate recorded music will help the children discover smooth and rhythmic patterns of movement.

Ways to Conclude the Session

The final part of the plan is to discover a suitable way to conclude the experience. Here are five ways that have worked for others:

[1]Adapted from Margaret Taylor, *Dramatic Dance with Children in Education and Worship,* Doug Adams, ed. (North Aurora, Ill.: The Sharing Company, 1977), p. 10.

1. Recall feelings. Ask the children to recall the strongest feeling they had as they danced in response to hearing the Bible story. They might then be encouraged to do one last movement to express that feeling.

2. Use round-robin storytelling. Retell the story in a round-robin fashion. The children should be seated in a circle; one person starts the story, the next adds to it, and so on, until everyone has had at least one turn, and the story is finished. This activity helps children relate the dance back to the story in an intentional way. It also gives them the opportunity to talk about any new insights they may have discovered about the passage through the experience of the dance.

3. Use worship. Ask the group to sit in a circle on the floor, clasping hands with the persons on either side of them. Lead them in thanking God, either silently or aloud, for the time shared in dance, and for the gift of movement God has given.

4. Review with the children how this experience relates to the lesson purpose for the day.

5. Reread the passage directly from the Bible.

And so the plan has been completed, starting with warm-ups that stimulated their imaginations, moving on to an experience of the Bible text itself, then to the dance portion of the session, and finally to a meaningful conclusion. With this plan in mind we now turn to the use of dance in relation to a specific Bible text.

Parable of the Lost Sheep (Luke 15:3-7)

The parable of the lost sheep is the story of a sheep that wanders away from the flock and of a concerned shepherd who searches to find it. With great joy the sheep finally is found and guided home. Like the concerned shepherd, God cares about each person. An exploration and expression of feelings is an appropriate response to this story. Two emotions are thrown into sharp contrast. The story begins with sadness and loss and moves on to joy and recovery. It finally concludes in a mood of praise and thanksgiving when it is realized that God is much like a concerned shepherd. Most children are not able to theologize about "joy in heaven" but they do know how happy they feel when they find a treasured object that has been lost, and they are able to feel awe and wonder as they catch a glimpse of what God is like.

A "Feeling Into" Warm-up

Ask the children to stand up and find a space where they will be able to move freely. Encourage them to imagine that they are sheep, grazing on a hillside covered with beautiful green grass. They are very, very small sheep. They run and jump and enjoy the warm sunshine overhead and the cool grass beneath their feet. Wherever they go they are careful to watch the shepherd (the teacher) because they know that getting lost is the worst thing that can happen to little sheep. Finally, when they have eaten enough, they fall fast asleep.

As the children follow the lead of your voice, a kind of follow-the-leader will take place. Through this activity their bodies have been prepared for movement about the room, and their imaginations have been stimulated so that they are prepared to hear the story.

"Meeting with" the Bible Passage

Gently "awaken the sheep," and gather them in a group around you.

"One day Jesus told a story about a sheep that wandered away from the rest of the flock and really did get lost."

You now have the rapt attention of a captive audience for your telling of the story.

Dance as a Response

Ask the children to become "statues" which are showing how it feels to be lost. Then encourage the "statues" to move in place, now showing how it feels to be found! Let the children repeat this change several times as they begin to feel the rhythm of lost-to-found. Next, suggest that they move about the room, perhaps expressing "lost" in one spot and moving smoothly to other places in the room to show the feeling of "found." After the pattern has been established, mood music will help with the flow of the dance.

Conclude the Session

Help the children use words to tell how it feels to be found after being lost, and close with a prayer of thanks that God cares about each person just as the shepherd cared about each sheep.

Tips for Teacher

In addition to mastering the basic principles presented in this section there are some very practical things you can do right away.

Begin to develop a collection of props: brightly colored scarves, crepe paper streamers, rhythm instruments, and balloons.

Make a set of large and easily read flash cards on which are written "-ing" and "-ly" words.

Start a music resource bank. On individual cassette tapes, record short bits of music, each expressing a different emotion—music that is sad, happy, carefree, lilting, angry, or peaceful. Also create recordings that contain music of contrasting moods on one tape or disc—for example, a tape on which sad music becomes happy music, and another that would help children move from angry feelings to a mood of serenity.

Above all, avoid the temptation to "show off" the dances the children have created. This may be possible later, if a group grows enthusiastic about dancing and wants to share with others; but to suggest performance too early is sure to result in some children "freezing up" rather than being "freed up"! Just as in creative drama, the process is more important than the product.

DIALOGUE

As human beings, we are distinguished from other creatures by our ability to invent and use language in both its spoken and written forms. Although body gestures can express many messages, it is through words that highly complex communication is possible. When communication is one-way, from teacher to child, it is called the lecture method. Communication during which teachers and students listen to each other with respect and with expectation of learning from each other may be referred to as dialogue. This might seem to be the least controversial teaching method, but it does not have total acceptance. Those who prefer the lecture approach often refer to discussion as a "pooling of ignorance." Others, who understand the need for children to be physically active, deplore time spent in what seems a passive activity. These criticisms stem not so much from a disagreement with the method itself as from the way it has been used.

Before the Dialogue

There are four conditions which need to be present in order for dialogue to be an effective way for teachers, parents, and children to respond to an experience of the Bible.

1. First, there must have been an experience worth responding to. If the "feeling into" and "meeting with" activities have been carried out effectively, there will be a

rich experience from which the child can respond. If not, the discussion will be superficial.

2. Even when the response activity is a discussion, it first needs to be at the feeling level. Often, we have treated biblical content as so many facts to be learned and repeated back to the teacher, rather than as an experience to be felt and expressed. We told the story of the Last Supper, and then engaged in conversation that went something like this:

Teacher: How many disciples were at the Last Supper?
Child: Twelve
Teacher: Good. What were their names?
Children: (Names are given with a good deal of prompting by the teacher.)
Teacher: Which disciple was not loyal to Jesus?
Children: (in chorus) Judas!
Teacher: Fine! That is right! What was Judas going to do?
Child: Betray Jesus.
Teacher: All right. But why did he want to do that?
Child: For money.
Teacher: Yes, but how much money?
Child: Thirty pieces of silver.
Teacher: Do you know how much money that would be today?

And so the interchange would go, on and on. Having drawn from the children all the right answers, the teacher concluded that they now knew the story.

But this sense of satisfaction was ill-founded. In this "lesson" there was no recognition of the anxiety the disciples felt about the growing animosity toward Jesus. Nor was there any room for the sorrow and guilt they must have felt when confronted with the thought that one of their own number would betray him. There was no sensitivity to the contrast between values—money or a life. And least of all was there any opportunity for the children to respond with their own feelings about the impending death of an innocent and good man.

Most computer Bible games are created using a right/wrong approach and are therefore effective when the teaching of Bible facts is the intended and stated purpose. But this is not dialogue, nor is this an effective way to encourage dialogue.

When the Bible is taught only as a series of factual right-or-wrong statements, it loses the power to capture a child's imagination and emotions. Commitment to becoming a follower of Jesus is not prompted by facts about an event, but by feelings about a person.

3. If response to the Bible is to be dialogue, both adults and children should share meanings and feelings, both should ask questions, and both should be active listeners. Serious responses should be considered seriously. Teachers who answer children with verbal or nonverbal language that says, "What a stupid comment!" should not be surprised when their further efforts at discussion prove unsatisfactory.

Many discussions are ineffective because adults respond to what they want to hear, rather than to what is actually being said. When children are conditioned to make certain responses, they may articulate the adult's response to the Bible text; they do not express their own reactions—they only express their desire to please the adult.

When children are helped to express their feelings about the Bible, a dialogue that reflects meaning is more apt to occur. Using this approach, a discussion of the Last Supper might sound like this:

Teacher: How do you feel about the story of Jesus eating supper with his disciples for the last time?

Child:	The supper was all right, but I didn't like the way it ended.
Teacher:	What do you mean, about the ending?
Child:	Well, that one of the disciples was a traitor. That made me sad.
Teacher:	That makes me sad, too. I've often wondered how the disciples felt when Jesus said one of them was going to betray him.
Child:	They probably wondered who it was.
Child:	They were probably afraid he meant them!
Child:	I think they must have been angry!
Teacher:	The disciples must have had a lot of mixed-up feelings. I hadn't thought about them being angry, though.
Child:	Well, *I'd* have been angry! Why did people want to kill Jesus? It wasn't fair!

The secret of teaching dialogically is the ability of the teacher to be present fully with the child. Here again the computer fails as a partner in dialogue. Although some programs allow a variety of responses, an absent programmer-technician can never engage in meaningful interaction with the child.

4. When dialogue is chosen as the way to help children respond to the Bible, the conversation should be kept within the limits of their intellectual ability. Often discussions end in failure and problems with discipline, not because children are inherently naughty, but because the conversation has left their concrete world and has taken on an abstraction to which they cannot relate.

"Why did people want to kill Jesus? It wasn't fair!" That is a question children can and want to discuss, because being fair is one of childhood's highest values. Attempts to discuss such abstract concepts as "suffering servant" and "atonement" are better left for their youth and adult years.

Summary

Whether or not children have learned the facts of a Bible text may be discovered by involving them in a discussion of the story, but discussion can achieve other results that are even more important. Through dialogue children can be helped to respond to the Bible honestly, at both the feeling level and the intellectual level. They can catch a sense of what it means to be members of the Christian community as they engage in serious reflection with the teachers and with one another about a significant part of the community's tradition. When their responses, however immature and fragmentary, have been taken seriously, they will be willing to share their thoughts again in the future.

DEED

Churchwide service projects are traditional at special seasons of the year; they may be initiated as part of a denominational or ecumenical program, or they may be in response to some immediate need. At these times children's groups are often asked to join in the total church effort. It is not always necessary to relate the project to a Bible story or text. It is enough to help children understand that the service project is the Church at work.

Although most service projects do not originate as a result of Bible study, some may, if concern for others and the desire to be of service seems the most appropriate response, and it is those projects we will discuss here.

Before You Initiate a Service Project

"Let's do a service project!" is more apt to be the spontaneous response to a "meeting with" the Bible if three conditions are present.

1. The Bible selection should have within it a challenge to service, if we expect children to respond in that way.

For example, the "As you did it to one of the least of these" passage (Matthew 25:34-45) calls for a service response much more than does the Twenty-third Psalm.

2. An already established atmosphere of caring and social action within the church or home will prompt children to think of service. If children have not seen the church or their parents at work for others, they are unlikely to respond to a Bible passage by suggesting such an action.

3. Older children are more likely to respond to Bible study by suggesting service. Service projects are most appropriate for younger children when there is an actual need that they can see. If children are personally acquainted with flood victims in their community, there is no need for a biblical rationale for service. Serving others is what Christians do. But the mental operations required to go from an ancient writing to a present-day meaning, and finally to an implication for action, can be performed only by older children, and even then with some difficulty.

When the atmosphere is supportive and the biblical text appropriate, older children may find a project of service to others the most natural response to make. For times like this, here are some specific suggestions.

Whatever the response children make, it should come from within their own feelings and understandings. If in your planning you think a service project would be a fitting response, the "feeling into" and "meeting with" phases of the lesson plan will need to be carefully prepared. Children may agree to a service project, but unless it is a spontaneous response, they may not have enough interest to complete it. When a project must be completed by the teachers, it is a sign that it was not really the children's project in the first place.

A decision to do a service project is unique. Other responses are open-ended. That is, a wide range of ideas and emotions can be expressed through dance, art, or discussion. To propose painting one's feelings is not to say what those feelings ought to be; it is only to suggest a way to express them. A service project, on the other hand, assumes not only that children have feelings, but that they have a particular feeling—a concern for others.

To avoid manipulating the responses of children, the decision to begin a service project should be preceded by thorough discussion. If the course of the discussion seems to warrant it, the teacher might ask, "What if we, right here in this church, took this Bible passage seriously? Is there anything we might do?" If there are no enthusiastic answers, it is obvious that for this group of children, a service project is not a natural response. But if ideas begin to flow, then such a project may be considered.

These questions will help you and your class choose a project: Does this project meet a real need? What would it mean in terms of time, skills, and money? Are we willing and able to put forth as much effort as will be needed? To obtain answers, the class may need to do some research. They may want to involve their parents or other church and community adults. When all the facts are in, the decision can be made.

Keeping the Project a Response to the Bible

A service project as a response to the Bible points in two directions. First, it points forward toward those it seeks to serve. It is a concrete action that meets a tangible need. It also points backward to the Bible passage itself, as it helps to reinforce the significance of the story for the children. For this reason it is important to maintain a link to the Bible passage until the project has been completed. Here are some ways this might be done.

1. Suggest that the children name the project to remind them of the Bible story—"The Inasmuch Project," "The Good Sam Club," or "The Second Milers."

2. Guide a committee of children in making a bulletin board on which they post appropriate Bible story pictures and pictures of the project as it progresses.

3. Help the children choose one phrase or verse from the Bible passage, and make a banner to be displayed in the classroom until the project is completed.

Concluding the Project

Several weeks may elapse between the Bible study and the completion of the project. Choose a way to conclude that will help the children recall the fun they had together as they worked on the project, and that will at the same time emphasize the importance of what they have accomplished. Perhaps you will plan a worship service or a party-type celebration. Guests may be invited who will share in reflecting on the events surrounding the project. Also included should be a recall of the Bible text that underlay the project.

Summary

A service project is one of the most complex responses children can make to a Bible passage. Thoughtful discussion should precede its selection; children should value it as their own choice; both need and practicability should be considered; and it should be followed through to a meaningful conclusion.

11.
DIMENSIONS OF RESPONSE AND MEANING

After children have experienced the Bible as Event, there are four levels at which they can begin to discover meanings. The first is, "What does it mean to me right now—as a child?" The second, "What does it mean to you—my teacher, parent, or adult friend?" The third, "What did it mean to them—the original storytellers and listeners?" And fourth, "What does it mean to us as members of the Christian church in the world today?"

"What Does It Mean to Me?"

The immediate response to any exciting event is at the personal meaning level. If the Bible is really an Event which is made to live, the experience will produce in children a wide range of possible meanings. Adults can aid the exploration and discovery of "What does it mean to me?" in three ways:

First, with children of all ages by being alert to hear meanings when they are expressed spontaneously. Such expression is our best clue as to how children are understanding the Bible.

Second, with early and older elementary children by asking questions and encouraging responses. Often this can be in a conversation or discussion group. A variety of questions can be asked:

What does the story mean to you?
What did the story say?
What did you like about the story?
Did it remind you of anything?
Whom did you like best? Why?

If you had been David, what would you have done? What did you think about the way the story ended? How else might it have ended?

Sometimes the response can be in written form. When asked to vote for the person she liked best in the story of the prodigal son, one child marked the ballot for the father and explained, "Because he understood that the boy had to go." Another voted for the son who stayed home as the character most disliked because "he was a spoiled brat!" Sometimes the meaning can be expressed in a poem or a story or a prayer.

At other times the response will include nonverbal forms. The teacher can suggest:

Paint a picture about the story.
Fingerpaint how the story made you feel.
Show how you think Moses felt by the way you stand or move around the room.
Act out the story using puppets.

And during these activities the teacher can be alert for clues that reveal how children have heard and are interpreting the biblical material.

Third, with children of all ages by allowing and accepting the meaning responses that are made. If we ask a guest in our home, "How is the temperature in the house for you?" and the guest responds honestly, the answer cannot be wrong. If he or she answers, "I am a little chilly" although the thermometer indicates eighty degrees, we cannot validly say "You are wrong. You aren't chilly." We can say that we ourselves are not chilly; we can show our guest the thermometer; we can offer articles that cite sixty-eight degrees as the ideal house temperature. But in no way can we deny the fact that our guest feels chilly. In fact, if we were not going to accept the answer given, the question should never have been asked.

Similarly, if children are asked what a Bible story means to them, the answer cannot be wrong. It may not match our own understanding or that of the Bible commentaries we have consulted. It may not seem adequate to us, but it is not wrong. If that is what the child understands, then that is what it means.

As the teacher asks the question and accepts the response, children begin to learn an important lesson: "The Bible is more than stories. It is a book that has meaning for the adults in my life, and they think it can have meaning for me, too." And when the responses of children are accepted in good faith, they begin to learn a second lesson, which is: "I can be a Bible interpreter, too."

There are some things we should not do. We can avoid questions that require predetermined answers. This practice results eventually in hypocrisy on the part of children because they tell us what they think we want to hear. When this happens, teachers and parents receive wrong data from the children.

We can avoid interpreting aloud a child's art work or other nonverbal responses. And we can avoid saying that children's meanings are wrong.

But no conscientious teacher will want to leave the process at this point for very long. Therefore, the teacher will move to the next meaning level, where the child asks, "Teacher, what does this Bible story mean to you?"

"What Does It Mean to You?"

To request and accept the meanings of children and to withhold our own is not only unfair, but it is to miss one of the most important teaching opportunities we have. In the same spirit with which we accepted the child's meaning response, we can now share our own. We do not do it to correct a wrong idea or to establish a standard by which children can evaluate their understandings, but we do it because we recognize the child as a member of the Christian community with whom we want to share our faith.

Our responses to the child's meaning statements may take varied forms. If the child expresses our own ideas we might respond with, "I think that, too. I wonder if there are boys and girls or teachers here who have a different idea to share with us?" If a child expresses a concept unlike our own, we can acknowledge the difference. We might respond, "That's a new idea! I've never thought about it like that before. To me it means. . . ." Or, "I used to think that, too. Now I think. . . ." When children are led to respond to biblical materials in nonverbal ways, such as drawing or using puppets, it is helpful if teachers have participated in these activities, also. This makes it possible for adults to share with children at both the verbal and nonverbal levels.

As a result of this mutual sharing, children may learn several things: "The important people in my life and I share something important. We both find meaning in the Bible." Or, "Even adults are still discovering new meanings in the Bible." Or, "It will be all right to change my mind later on."

Helping children find Bible meanings does not stop with the personal meanings of children and their teachers.

"What Did It Mean to Them?"

Part of our teaching task is to help children know that the Bible and its stories had meaning for people a long time ago, too. With some early elementary children and with older elementary children we can raise the question, "I wonder what this story meant to the very first people who ever heard it?" or "I wonder why people thought this story was so important that they wrote it down?"

Here again the most important point is not to teach the

right answer, although teachers will want to consult Bible commentaries to discover what answers may be given there. The important thing is to help children realize that the Bible did not just happen, that real people told the stories because they had found meaning in the events in the stories, that there was purpose in the minds of those who retold and wrote down the stories, that real people heard the stories and from the beginning real people have found meaning in them. In this way the dialogue is broadened from the child and you (the adult), to include them (the first storytellers and listeners).

"What Does It Mean to Us?"

"Us" here refers to the Christian church at this particular time in history. Older elementary boys and girls can begin to think about the relationship between our biblical heritage and the mission of the church in the world today. What does a particular story mean if taken seriously by the Christian community? In response we do not state a final answer, but we share our insights with one another.

By the time children reach this level of meaning discovery, an important thing has happened. The understanding of meaning has gone from a distinctly personal one that is based in present experience, to a dialogue of meaning with contemporary adult Christians, to a dialogue with the Bible writers in the past, and now returns to the present with a wider view of the whole world today. In the process the child's understanding of the Bible has expanded so that it is seen not only in individual terms, but in terms of "me" in relation to other Christians.

A movement through these four levels of meaning during the elementary years paves the way for exploration of a fifth level of meaning in adolescence: "What has the Bible meant to us (the church) historically?" Here the complicated study of heresies, councils, theological systems, and creeds can be begun with the recognition that the effort to find and express Bible meanings continues into adult life.

APPENDIX

"We Lived the Story"*

This is how one teaching team helped children experience the Bible from Advent to Easter to first Christians.

The curriculum for our first and second graders outlined eighteen Sundays—from Advent to Easter—on Jesus and three more on the first Christians. Our teaching team was not sure it could be done. With units of only four to six weeks in length, the children's interest had wavered. Little carry-over had occurred. How could these children ever experience the chronological flow of Jesus' life or grasp the meaning of the crucial events which brought the Christian church into being? But—we decided to try!

Experience was the key, we knew. The children's attention span as a group was about five minutes long. They ignored the book corner. They liked the mechanics of the projectors and record players, but we were not sure how much content they had learned. They loved to paint, to make things, to play, to do; but they were very shy about any activity which called upon them to perform.

Somehow, through paint, construction, play, and action, we needed to help them *experience* Jesus' birth, childhood, adulthood; his ministry, death, resurrection; and the beginnings of the Christian church. To achieve this goal would be to build a sound foundation for later serious study.

With this goal and the children in mind, our team began to plan. We agreed to change the room and activities frequently. We chose as sub-units:

Advent/Christmas (5 weeks)
Childhood Days (5 weeks)
Adulthood/Ministry (4 weeks)
Palm Sunday/Easter (3 weeks)
First Christians (3 weeks)

*Written by Mary Jo Osterman. Description of a first and second grade class, First United Methodist Church, Evanston, Illinois.

Advent/Christmas

On the first Sunday in Advent, the children were greeted with a sign which announced "Christmas Is Coming." In each corner of the room, the scene was set: an inn, a stable nearby, a shepherds' hillside, and a desert in a far corner. Each scene was labeled with a bright poster. And everywhere, the large yellow star shone.

Each Sunday a different part of the Christmas story was emphasized—through filmslip, song, verse, creche—and then "worked on" in the room. A manger was made; cows, donkeys, sheep, and camels painted. As the scenes came alive weekly, props were added, such as costumes, a baby doll, and shepherds' staffs.

An art worktable attracted some children with more developed muscle control (and some with too much inhibition to work in the large scenes). Art work corresponded to the emphasis of the morning.

Our theme song became "Hey! Hey! Anybody Listening?"[1] It was sung each Sunday with guitar and rhythm instruments.

The three teachers moved among the children to encourage their actions and conversations informally. We hoped for that spark which would kindle imaginations and overcome self-consciousness so the children could *really be* Mary and Joseph, the shepherds, wise men, and innkeeper. Halfhearted attempts were made, with teachers directing the pantomime, but real identification did not occur.

However, evaluation of this first sub-unit was positive: the children had somewhat experienced the birth event of Jesus' life. And the teachers had glimpsed a teaching style that could bring the Christian story alive for children.

Childhood Days

With a quick change of scenery, children were next greeted by the sign—"And Jesus Grew." Our room had become the town of Nazareth, with Jesus' home, a marketplace, a synagogue, and a well-stocked carpenter's shop.

We introduced the Childhood Days sub-unit, and built on the Christmas unit, through the use of the song "And Jesus Grew":

[1] Words and Music by Richard K. Avery and Donald S. Marsh, *Middle Elementary Student,* Winter 1977–78, Graded Press.

1. He was born and laid in a manger
   There were shepherds and kings who came,
   And he had around him a family,
   And Jesus grew.

2. Now his father was Joseph, a carpenter
   And he worked with his tools and woods,
   And Mary cared for her infant son,
   And Jesus grew.[2]

To our amazement, one child responded, "But Jesus was never a little boy like me—he didn't grow like me!" The faces of others indicated agreement: Jesus was different—maybe like Superman? Somehow we had to help these children experience Jesus as a growing child just like themselves.

As the children moved freely about the room, early Bible-time activities were suggested by word, by pictures, by art, and by construction materials. Soon a large boat was being built; sandals, coins, and bowls were created; bread was baked and butter made; sand writing and scroll making were carried on and mezuzahs made. Scenery painting flourished everywhere.

Each Sunday we began with the song "And Jesus Grew," and composed our own verses about the children's activities. Soon we had added:

3. He went to the market with Joseph
   They took coins—bronze, silver and gold,
   And they bought a clay bowl and some sandals,
   And Jesus grew.

4. Now he went to school at the synagogue;
   He learned reading and writing there.
   He prayed to God and he worshiped, too,
   And Jesus grew.

[2] From "And Jesus Grew," verses 1, 2, and 5 by Ann F. Price. Words and music copyright © 1973 by Graded Press. Verses 3, 4, 6, 7, 8, and 9 were composed by Dorothy Jean Furnish. From *The I-II Teacher*, Winter 1974–75, p. 87. Copyright © 1974 by Graded Press.

5. He went to the priests at the Temple;
   He listened so carefully.
   He questioned them and thought on it.
   And Jesus grew.

Informal conversations continued: "Let's finish this bread and go to the marketplace. I need some new sandals today." Teachers self-consciously stopped to "buy" a clay bowl with a bronze coin or became sellers in the marketplace. Some giggly, sporadic role-playing began to take place by the children also.

Each Sunday, the sessions ended in the synagogue with a brief worship in the Jewish style, lighting the candle with four wicks, reading verses from scrolls, saying "Shalom" and "The Lord bless and keep you."

Adulthood/Ministry

One Sunday in February, after four weeks immersion in childhood activities and life in a village, the children were greeted with a new sign "And Jesus Was Grown UP!" The room now held a seashore (with the boat tied up at water's edge), Mary and Martha's home, the Temple, and the marketplace.

The teaching team added a new member, a seminary student who agreed to "be" the grown-up Jesus. Wearing Christmas pageant robe and old sandals, he wandered around the room, engaged children in conversation, and told stories.

On the first Sunday of this sub-unit, "Jesus" was baptized by John the Baptist in the River Jordan (butcher paper rolled across the floor). Children were "baptized" in the river throughout the morning. Another Sunday, teachers acted out a playlet called "Jesus Visits Mary and Martha at Bethany" (a modern paraphrase by one of the teachers). Later, Jesus replayed the story with the children.

In the marketplace, buying and selling began in earnest. At the seashore, net-making was popular. A teacher in costume conversed about "this man Jesus who told stories and talked about loving our enemies and doing good." Jesus' disciples were introduced, and each child became one—except for several girls who decided to become Jesus' mother, or Elizabeth or Mary or Martha!

By this time we had added the next two verses to our song:

6. He went to the river Jordan.
   He found John the Baptizer there;
   And he said to John, "Please baptize me."
   And Jesus was grown UP.

7. Jesus went to the seashore,
   He saw boats and fishermen, too.
   And he called and said "Come, follow me."
   And Jesus was grown UP.

One Sunday, conversation shifted toward a discussion of people who did not like Jesus. Jesus talked about taking a trip to Jerusalem.

Palm Sunday/Easter

Near the end of the session before Palm Sunday, butcher paper was rolled across the room to the Temple. Jesus gathered his disciples and friends for the trip. A crowd stood along the road and waved paper palm branches. Jesus walked the road, stopped to talk, waved. Everyone gathered at the Temple for worship and a new verse was added to our song:

8. Jesus went to Jerusalem.
   The crowds were glad that he came.
   And they waved palm branches and sang "Hosanna."
   And Jesus was grown UP.

On Palm Sunday the children distributed palm fronds in church. They sang "And Jesus Grew" for the congregation prior to the sermon, then returned to their learning center to continue "living" the story. Again, the Palm Sunday trip was played, this time with real palm fronds carefully "saved" from church! At the close of the session the last verse was introduced:

9. Now Jesus had some enemies.
   They had him put to death.
   But on Easter Day his friends all know
   That Jesus Lives On!

The events of the coming passion week were discussed. The children attended church with their parents on Easter Sunday to celebrate the fact that "Jesus Lives On!"

The First Christians

After Easter, the room looked just the same, but "Jesus" was gone. Conversations change: "Good News: Jesus is still alive." "Remember when Jesus told us the story about . . ." "The Roman soldiers questioned me in the marketplace today." "Let's meet tonight at Mary and Martha's, but be careful not to let anyone see you. Make the sign of the fish when you knock."

The next Sunday, Mary and Martha's house had a fourth wall for a secret meeting place. A jail stood in another corner. A tunnel led to the catacombs (formerly the coatroom).

A teacher with guitar sang with the Christians who were put in jail by Roman soldiers. Christians painted on the walls about Jesus and God; "non-Christians" painted "I hate Jesus."

Wire fish symbols were worn by Christians to gain entrance to a night meeting, which was a hurried, silent meal of matzo crackers and grape juice. A disciple watched for soldiers who stomped the streets. The Christians stole silently across "town" to the catacombs for a secret worship meeting. (The role-playing came naturally; teachers guided by their own participation.)

At the end of one secret catacomb meeting a child read a scroll which announced that "Emperor Constantine has become a Christian and now Christians do not have to hide anymore. " A spontaneous cheer rose from the children hidden in the catacombs. Talk began about "building our own church to worship in."

We Lived "The Story"

From December through April, we lived the story of Jesus. Our beginning halfhearted role-playing efforts had borne fruit—the children had become Mary and Martha, Jesus and the disciples, the early Christians and the Roman soldiers! They had played and worked in Nazareth! They had fished and listened to Jesus by the seashore! They had waved and cheered by the roadside! They had feared in the jails and catacombs because they had tried to share the "good news" about Jesus! They had shouted their joy for the freedom to worship openly!

We Used the Three Guidelines

This experiential approach to teaching the Bible used each of the guidelines presented earlier.

Guideline One: "Feeling into"

The physical environment of the room helped the children "feel into" the story of Jesus' life in an indirect way. Children entered the ministages and worked on activities initially on the basis of their here-and-now interest in such things as painting, working with clay, or pounding nails into wood. These activities drew upon their senses and imaginations and feelings, to prepare them for experiencing some of the same emotions as the biblical people who had lived in those scenes. As children finished constructing the scenery for the ministages and entered into the other activities of that setting (such as net-making in the seashore scene), they began to "own" the scenes and to move into and live in them.

A second type of "feeling into" activity involved the role-playing of the teachers. The children were able to make the scenes their own, mainly because of the teachers' informal portrayal of biblical characters in the midst of these scenes. The teachers' one-line verbal interactions helped the children connect their here-and-now interests and feelings with the past. For example, when a teacher, role-playing a new Christian, said, "The Roman soldiers questioned me in the marketplace today," that teacher was in effect "hooking" the children's feelings of fear and anxiety toward aggressive, authoritarian persons. The children were able to respond to this bit of the story with the same feelings, thoughts, and actions as those of a biblical person, because the feelings were familiar to them in their real world.

Guideline Two: "Meeting with"

Formal ways of presenting the biblical story were planned by the teachers. These "meeting with" activities included: the telling of the Christmas story in a different way at the beginning of each Advent session; the singing of "And Jesus Grew" at the beginning of each session during the childhood and adult units on Jesus' life; the role-playing by the teachers in the skit about

Mary and Martha; the reading of the scroll about Constantine by the child in the catacombs.

Semiformal ways of presenting the story also were planned. However, these ways involved much improvisation on the part of teachers and children during the session: the wandering "Jesus" telling parables to the children; the parade on Palm Sunday; the hurried meal, followed by the silent stealing across town to the catacombs.

Informal ways of presenting the story were sometimes planned in a general sense, but more often they were spontaneous. Teachers improvised with the children both verbal and nonverbal interactions appropriate to the situations and in this way disclosed bits and pieces of the biblical story. Children also met with some of the story each time they walked into their classroom and absorbed the story revealed by the ministages.

Guideline Three: "Responding out of"

In the example, two kinds of children's responses can be identified—thinking responses and spontaneous feeling-and-acting responses.

Thinking responses occurred in several places. The children "met with" a portion of the biblical story of Jesus' life when the teachers sang the first two verses of the song "And Jesus Grew." The child's reaction was a thinking response: "But Jesus was never a little boy like me." Another kind of thinking response occurred when the teachers discussed the events of Passion Week with the children and briefly explored the significance of singing, "But on Easter Day his friends all know that Jesus lives on."

Spontaneous feeling-and-acting responses occurred throughout the various subunits on Jesus. When the two children who had worked hardest on the boat finally finished the sails and oars, they climbed into the boat, surveyed the room with smiles of satisfaction, then climbed out and went on to other activities. The children's silence during the secret meal and their sneaking across town to the catacombs were feelings translated into actions. So was the noisy aggressive stomping of those children who became Roman soldiers. Feeling responses were also evident in the graffiti written on the walls of the jail. Finally, the spontaneous cheer of the Christians hidden in the catacombs was perhaps the ultimate indication that the children were feeling the emotions of the early Christians and were responding from deep within themselves to the total environment of their classroom.

Summary

Within this total-environment approach, the guidelines become fluid processes, rather than three distinct types of activities with discernible beginnings and endings. "Feeling-into" moments occur many times for the children throughout the session. These times often flow into the "meeting-with" processes without distinguishable breaks. Finally, because they are moving and choosing freely, the children in the room are free to create their own responses at any time.

Selected Bibliography

Cavelletti, Sophia. *Religious Potential of the Child*. New York: Paulist Press, 1983.

Elkind, David. *The Child's Reality: Three Developmental Themes*. Hillsdale, N.J.: L. Erlbaum, 1978.

Fowler, James. *Stages of Faith: The Psychology of Human Development and the Quest for Meaning*. San Francisco: Harper & Row, 1981.

Gobbel, A. Roger. *The Bible, A Child's Playground*. Philadelphia: Fortress Press, 1986.

Griggs, Patricia. *Opening the Bible with Children: Beginning Bible Skills*. Nashville: Abingdon Press, 1986. (A Griggs Educational Resource).

Smith, Judy Gattis. *Teaching to Wonder: Spiritual Growth Through Imagination and Movement*. Nashville: Abingdon Press, 1989. (A Griggs Educational Resource)

Westerhoff, John H., III. *Will Our Children Have Faith?* New York: Seabury Press, 1976.